7-27-23

Lonnie + Beth

Thank you for your friendship, love, great wisdom and always an example of God's Love.

Much Love,
Lonnie

"Feed People"

"Feed People"

Donna Rollyson

XULON PRESS

Xulon Press
2301 Lucien Way #415
Maitland, FL 32751
407.339.4217
www.xulonpress.com

© 2023 by Donna Rollyson

Contribution by: Darla Columbo

All rights reserved solely by the author. The author guarantees all contents are original and do not infringe upon the legal rights of any other person or work. No part of this book may be reproduced in any form without the permission of the author.

Due to the changing nature of the Internet, if there are any web addresses, links, or URLs included in this manuscript, these may have been altered and may no longer be accessible. The views and opinions shared in this book belong solely to the author and do not necessarily reflect those of the publisher. The publisher therefore disclaims responsibility for the views or opinions expressed within the work.

Unless otherwise indicated, Scripture quotations taken from the New King James Version (NKJV). Copyright © 1982 by Thomas Nelson, Inc. Used by permission. All rights reserved.

Paperback ISBN-13: 978-1-66287-933-3
Ebook ISBN-13: 978-1-66287-934-0

Table of Contents

Part I: "When God Speaks...Listen" 1
    How God Works 3
    "Feed People" 5
    The Dream! 9

Part II: "The Dream Team" 19
    We Meet 21
    My Beautiful Savannah 25
    The Need For Fellowship 32
    Building a Business 36

Part III: God's Calling Upon Our Lives 47
    My Calling 49
    Ed's Calling 52
    A Time of Testing 58
    Activating the Call 62
    A Lesson In Obedience 66

Part IV: Help Wanted: The Dream Team is needed in West Virginia ... 73
    Heading Back To Savannah 75
    Let the Work Begin – August 1, 2020 78
    Selling Our Savannah Home 85
    "Feed People"- Opening a Food Pantry 91
    Spruce Grove Community Church Opens 97

Part V: The Beginning of God's Magnificence!......................103
    Feeding People – God Style 105
    God Fulfills His Promise................................... 111
    Staying the Course 122

Part I
"When God Speaks... Listen"

How God Works

HAVE YOU EVER experienced a direct word from God? It settles deep into your spirit as direct instructions from the Creator of all things. The Author of life has spoken to YOU! He whispered into your inner ear a special command that simply cannot be ignored. He has a plan that only you can complete; only you can accomplish this very specific task. Having heard His initial voice, you lean in, listen for further instruction, wait, and anticipate the next directive.

One of my favorite things to do is study the Word of God. In doing so, I read about the various characters whose entire lives are changed when God spoke to them and altered their course in life. One of my favorites is the story of Abraham, or Abram, as his story begins.

One day Abram is living in the land of Haran, the place of his father's family, and God speaks to him, "Get out of your country, from your family and from your father's house to a land that I will show you". (Genesis 12:1) Scripture goes on to say that Abram departed as the Lord had told him. There is no record of long goodbyes with his father or extended family nor is there written a struggle with what to do or where to go. No recorded conversations are found that he had with his wife as to where they might be going and why. By all accounts, it was immediate. God spoke into the heart of Abram; he heard it and immediately gathered up his wife and belongings and began his journey. Where? To a land I will show you! God would show him when he arrived that he had reached the desired destination. I absolutely love the trusting and obedient heart of Abram. His heart was in tune with the magnificent God who revealed himself in such a way, that without question, he did as he was instructed.

God spoke deep into Abram's heart. Long before there were churches, tabernacles, or even the written word, God revealed Himself to this man named Abram. In that moment when He spoke to him, there was little doubt in Abram that he would immediately follow God's instructions. Later, Abram would become Abraham and at such a time was promised to become a father of many nations. He was promised to be exceedingly fruitful, and nations and kings would come from him.

Abraham would not live long enough to see all that God had planned to do through him, as this plan would last through the ages. He believed this vast futuristic promise that his descendants would be like the stars in the sky. He would die long before the nation of Israel would be formed from his linage of sons, long before kings would walk the desert land with his bloodline attached to his name. But what Abraham had that would set him apart, that brought such favor in the eyes of God Almighty, was his faith, a faith in the One who spoke to him and told him things that would come to be. Abram heard, believed, and followed the command to leave his father's house and go to a land in which God wanted his people to reside.

Abram, having heard the heart of God, had a special connection with God, a friendship.

"But you, Israel, are My servant, Jacob whom I have chosen, the descendants of Abraham MY FRIEND." (Isaiah 41:8)

"Feed People"

MY STORY IS not much different. Out of nowhere God gave me a two-worded instruction, "Feed people." That is all it was. These two words had a clear concept of what was expected, to provide food for people. Specifics on how to accomplish that were not included in the command. Regardless, I knew I was given specific instructions and would immediately explore ways to fulfill the words God spoke to me.

The church where we attended in Savannah, Georgia, had a wonderful fellowship area with a fully equipped kitchen. Additionally, there were showers in each restroom which flooded my thoughts of how we could attend to the overcrowded homeless population in our community. My entrepreneur mind had it all worked out on how to develop a feeding program beyond our little food pantry that existed for emergency use only. The church campus was perfect for all the thoughts running through my head. The ideas were flooding my mind on how I could take the instruction from the Lord and create an amazing outreach program in the facility where we attended church.

I took my two-worded instructions from the Lord to the pastor. He expressed no interest in furthering what the church was already providing. They were set up as an emergency pantry, primarily for the homeless population that could stop in for a quick, easy to-go meal. His words "I don't know how to facilitate that" was somewhat of an aggravation at the time. However, I knew what God had instructed me to do; but what I didn't realize was that

He was preparing to relocate us, and that this was not the location where I would "feed people".

I also spoke to a few of my friends that attended our church. It was at this time that I found out one of our dear friends was a constant supplier of food to one of the recovery ministries in the area. Each month they would receive a list of items needed. They would head out to the local Sam's Club and gather all the items, and I am sure they would add to their list with extras.

This couple, who were in their early 70's, were unable to volunteer as they did in their younger years. Yet, they still found a way to support the great need to serve the addicted and homeless population that flooded the area. I might add, this kind of support doesn't just feed those who are hungry but is a much-needed backbone support to those on the frontlines in these ministries. Many times, they are not sure how they are going to swing the current obligation but isn't that how God works?! He uses one set of committed "hands and feet" to supply and support another set of "hands and feet". Only through the commitment of believers with an ear towards heaven and willingness to obey the instructions from God, does this happen.

My ideas of implementing a feeding program where we were currently serving quickly diminished. I couldn't seem to generate anyone to come along side of me or even help open the door to using what I thought was the perfect facility. In fact, we had a few rather disappointing events happen that solidified the intent of our current place of worship.

One Sunday morning the announcement was made that the food pantry was running low, and any items brought in would be welcomed. We immediately went out the following day and bought a trunk load of food for the pantry: items such as fruit cups, chili, Vienna sausages, and foods that could be easily opened and eaten without the requirement of cookware. My husband would always insist on providing a bulk package of vienna sausages. He has a vivid memory of a time in his life when he was homeless and living the life of a drug addict. That little can of sausages tasted like the best thing in the world. These little cans could hold the very same emotion for another homeless wanderer. However, our effort in providing boxes of food that day were left on the front table of the fellowship hall, where we were instructed to leave them for well over a month. There they sat, every day, for weeks as we worked on an outside project around the church facility. I had even asked if I could put them on the shelf in the pantry, but my offer was declined.

Very clearly our provisions were not going to feed the homeless that might stop in or even be put on the shelf. They were just left to set. This act of dismissing our gift was hurtful. The previous public announcement requesting these items seemed to be an invalid request since nothing was done with them once they were brought to the facility. But the statement made during an online announcement about not having need of any more Vienna sausages would appear to be a direct insult to our offering. These small disappointments were added to other little issues, that when the time came, made it slightly easier to leave when the Lord would lead us in another direction.

Ed and I had many discussions that, one day we would be the ones who would be in leadership and have the role and responsibility on how we responded to people's thoughts, ideas, and even actions. We began praying for the Lord's sensitivity towards the needs of others. "Lord, I pray that we do our best to get it right, and when we don't, correct us with Your wisdom, Your love, and Your guidance. Encourage anyone we may unintentionally hurt or discourage, and help them choose, as we did, to forgive and move on. We fully understand forgiveness is not easy at times, but it is required according to Your Word."

"For if you forgive men their trespasses, your heavenly Father will also forgive you. But if you do not forgive men their trespasses, neither will your Father forgive your trespasses."
Matthew 6: 14-15

The Dream!

NOT LONG AFTER my instructions to "feed people", God gave me a dream that would forever change our lives. This dream takes place solely in the sanctuary of a little country church. I knew it was a country church by the size and the general feel of the place. It was quaint and welcoming with white bead board walls, high ceiling, two simple sections of pews, and one aisle down the middle that ended at the altar.

In the dream I was standing up front facing the congregation which partially filled the pews. I was to the right-hand side of the pulpit as if I was a part of a group in the choir. I do believe my position in this dream is important. I am not the preacher but to the right which lends support. Everyone was singing "Hark the Harold Angels Sing". Suddenly, the rapture takes place! Half of the people disappear, simply vanish. But what was very interesting was that all the people on the left side of where I was standing were now gone along with the pews. The only thing remaining was little piles of dust scattered across the old wooden floor. In the time that it took for me to question "why am I still here?", I also vanished and became a part of those raptured. It is at this time I was awakened in an abrupt way, having remembered every single aspect of the dream, as I still do to this day. In fact, sitting on the right side of the front pew was a man whose face is still etched in my memory. His features were like many of the men in this area. His hair was medium brown and nearly hit his shoulder in length with a full dark beard. I've met a few men that resemble this man, whose face is the only one throughout the entire dream with any clarity. I have yet to meet the one who took first row center on the right-hand side of the church.

I do recall feeling a presence to my right. I don't know if that was because I was a part of a choir, or maybe the Lord Himself was standing next to me in church that Sunday, as a dream interpreter had suggested. After awakening from the dream, I found my husband on the back patio talking to his mom on the phone. She had just been visiting us after an eight-month journey across the United States. Upon arriving home, she found that her bathroom floor was collapsing and was discussing with my husband if he would consider coming to West Virginia to make the much-needed repairs. We took into consideration our current work schedule, our ministerial courses that were underway, and then began to make a plan to clear three or four weeks to go to West Virginia to make the needed repairs to Susie's bathroom.

Three months after the dream, we made our way to West Virginia. Our first stop was in Lewisburg, where my parents were living, and we visited them for a few days. Next, we traveled to Susie's on Monday and began demolition of the bathroom on Tuesday. Day three after we arrived and started the demo, we stopped and prepared a shopping list for the first stage of repairs.

No longer in the convenient city of Savannah, shopping for supplies took on a whole new meaning in this rural area of West Virginia. Regardless of the busy day of shopping, we still planned to meet Uncle Jim and Aunt Vera at Pizza Hut for their lunch buffet. At the last minute we found out that Pizza Hut was still closed due to COVID. It was mid-June of 2020 when all this was happening and COVID still had areas shut down or not operating at full capacity.

Instead, we stopped in at Minney's Diner, the only place to eat in Frametown. As we pulled in, I noticed an older gentleman sitting in his car who looked our way. As we got out, we greeted one another. He introduced himself as Herman Jones, a Methodist minister from Anstead. He looked at my husband and hope entered his face. He was searching for help unloading some furniture and had been inside the restaurant asking every man present if they would be willing to help him. He had yet to find the willing, able bodies needed to unload the heavy furniture that was on its way. He proceeded to ask Ed if he was available to help him for a few bucks. Herman and Susie sparked up a conversation about the place where we needed to go. Susie knew the exact location where he had described, and in the few minutes of conversation, we had made arrangements to meet at 12:30 at Spruce Grove Church.

This gave us just enough time to go inside, eat some lunch, and then head over the hill to the meeting place where we had agreed to assist this minister of the Word. As soon as we took the hard right off the little country road onto the even smaller gravel road, I received a whisper from the Lord. "This is the church of your dreams." Since I have already told you the dream, you know that at no point was I standing on the outside of this church. That did not matter. God shared with me that I was about to enter the dream that he had given me months ago.

I told my husband as we got out of the car what God had just shared with me. Honestly, I think he had forgotten all about the dream. He had tired of hearing me talk about it within those first few weeks. I had shared it with everyone that would listen because it had impacted me so strongly. And now according to this second whisper into my spirit, I was preparing myself to see what God had revealed to me in that dream three months earlier.

The truck and trailer that had hauled all the heavy furniture had been backed up to the front steps of this little country church. I made my way around the trailer and the few men that were gathered nearby. I felt as if I had nudged a few men to the side because I couldn't wait. Was I really going to see the church that I dreamed about just three months ago?

As I stepped through the foyer of the church, I noticed that all the pews were on one side and the other side was empty. Nothing but little piles of dust scattered across the old, wooded floor, just like the dream. I made my way to the platform and took my place, the same place where I stood for the entirety of my dream that would forever change my life. I stood and looked out over the room. It appeared just as it did at the tail end of my dream, the left side empty with nothing but little piles of dirt across the floor. I took a picture and immediately sent it to my sister and my mom declaring, "I am currently standing in the middle of my dream". My sister was the first to respond with "that's a little creepy", and I would have to admit it certainly had my full attention.

God whispered into my ear "This is the church of your dream".

The Dream!

Exactly as my dream.... Nothing but little piles of dust!

As I was clearly having a moment with the Lord, Susie started to come through the side door and was making her way to the platform. She had heard about my dream and could testify that it was exactly as I had stated months before. My husband would admit much later that it rather annoyed him that I was talking so much about this dream. I seemed to want to tell everyone that I had a dream about the rapture that took place inside a little country church. But at this very moment where I am standing in the exact spot that the dream took place, it became a form of validation that God had clearly orchestrated this event. From the dream months earlier, to our cancelled lunch plans with family, to Happy Herman sitting outside the local diner praying and asking the Lord for help in unloading all this heavy furniture. I now knew that every single bit of this was a God-designed appointment. The only question left was, "What was God's plan in orchestrating these months of events to get us to this little church?" As with Abraham, God had a plan. Could God be calling us into our own faith journey as He's done with so many of His followers over the years? One thing is for certain, as I stood on that stage overlooking what was placed in my mind's eye months before, God had my full undivided attention.

Have you ever experienced a moment in time where you knew beyond a shadow of a doubt that your life was going to change? FOREVER! At this very moment I had no idea what would transpire, but I had a brief and intense conversation with the Lord. I told Him that He had my attention, and I was all ears. Whatever He wanted, I would do, even if that meant moving from my beloved Savannah, Georgia, back to West Virginia.

I took a quick tour of this old country church. The floor was wavy and weak in spots, and the ceiling tiles were falling and stained throughout from obvious roof issues. There were areas to be avoided all together because one might fall through the weakened floor. The reason there were no pews on the left-hand side of the church was the eight-inch drop from where the floor was supposed to be due to failed floor joists. We wouldn't find out until much later that those endearing piles of dust scattered across the beautiful oak floor was the termite activity destroying the undercarriage of this lovely old church.

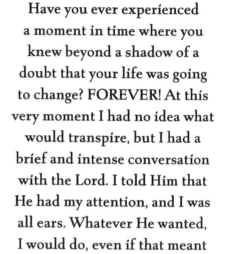

Have you ever experienced a moment in time where you knew beyond a shadow of a doubt that your life was going to change? FOREVER! At this very moment I had no idea what would transpire, but I had a brief and intense conversation with the Lord. I told Him that He had my attention, and I was all ears. Whatever He wanted, I would do, even if that meant moving from my beloved Savannah, Georgia, back to West Virginia.

There was, however, one room in the entire building that showed promise, the kitchen. Most likely this was the last addition made to the old building as it appeared somewhat fresher and newer than the 130-year-old original portion of the church. Immediately I thought of those two words.... "Feed People." Was this part of God's master plan in bringing us here, thru the dream, to fulfill His plan?

The Dream!

The following weeks my head would spin, as I tried to understand what God wanted to tell me. Did He really want us to leave our beautiful Savannah, the city of my dreams, to move back to West Virginia to this rural area where little opportunity existed for many of the folks in this county? Then I remembered the previous winter when prophetic words were spoken to me, while visiting a friend who lived near my parents in Lewisburg.

My friend Cinthia is a gifted daughter of the Most High King who has the ability to know certain things before they happen. I am not sure how she speaks these things, either with full knowledge that she is giving a prophetic word or that it is just part of her spirit's connection to our Heavenly Father. In casual conversation she stated to me, "When you move back to West Virginia". I was quick to let her know that I had no intention of moving back to West Virginia. I live in Savannah, Georgia, and that is exactly where I intended to stay. She turned to me and with a tilt of her head, a raised eyebrow, and that look that says, "If you say so," indicating she knew something I did not.

I also recall in that conversation, that I said God would have to give me a hand-written letter for me to move back to West Virginia. Well, He certainly did better than that. First, He gave me a dream and then placed me square in the middle of that dream just a few months later. There was no doubt God had something in mind when He planted that seed in us, long before any of these other things would come about.

In my 50 plus years on this earth, I have failed more often than recorded successes. I have not followed through with things the Lord had wanted me to do many times in the past. I recall having felt a call on my life when I was 16 to become a missionary. The Church of the Nazarene where my parents spent their life serving has always been huge on missions. Every month would be a country or segment that would let us know what was going on around the world regarding the mission field. I failed to follow through when I left college to get married the first time around. However, this was a clear opportunity because I knew for certain God had something specific for me to do. He had been abundantly clear with the message of "Feed People", vividly showing me the dream, leading me to meet Happy Herman, and revealing this little country church. Surely, He had more in store with all His master planning.

As I began to earnestly pray about what was next and what He wanted, He spoke one final message into my heart. "Something MAGNIFICIENT will happen in this church". That did it! I shared with Ed all my thoughts that had been swirling for days since that first introduction to this little church. He admitted feeling the pull and call as well. We agreed that if something were ever going to happen in this little country church, it would first have to be repaired and made useful again. That would require the "Dream Team", a fun title we gave ourselves in our handyman business we had while in Savannah.

The "Dream Team" would head to Savannah long enough to purchase a cargo trailer to load up all our tools and a few other necessities. Then we would head back to West Virginia to this little country church that was crumbling from neglect and disrepair. Our God still had claim on this old church, where through the years many had made life changing commitments. There was much more to be done within the walls of this old building and many more lives to be touched and affected by God's saving grace. But first, the dream team was needed.... Required!

God's desire to breathe new life into this old church would need someone willing to take on the decaying old building. No doubt the "Dream Team" was who God had called, and possibly even created for such a time as this.

Packed with tools and essentials to repair the little church in the valley.

Part II
"The Dream Team"

We Meet...

THE "DREAM TEAM" got its start on a little porch just outside of Clarksburg, West Virginia. One evening Ed, drunk and high on weed, started playing one of his favorite gospel songs, "Amazing Grace." He set the phone to his favorite bluegrass version, his hand reached for mine, and these two inebriated lovers began to sing and sway to the sounds of one of the most beloved hymns of all time.

> *"Amazing grace, how sweet the sound,*
> *That saved a wretch like me.*
> *I once was lost but now I am found,*
> *Was blind but now I see."*

I have often thought about those early days of how we started. Ed, a multiple offender of the law and a drug addict, was lost in a depraved state of living. I, a preacher's daughter, divorcee, and an alcoholic, was broken and battered by life's twists and turns. Somehow our paths crossed by means of internet dating, and our two lost souls found each other.

I truly believe that night, while swaying to the most well-known hymn of all time, God looked down and with a smile on his face, put a plan in place to give these two a purpose, a dream, and a desire for a better life. However, much would have to change before we could be any use to anyone, but God can take any mess and turn it into a masterpiece. In fact, I believe this to be His specialty.

"For we are God's masterpiece. He has created us a new in Christ Jesus, so we can do the good things he planned for us long ago."
Ephesians 2:20

During the summer months of 2016, we met and dated with a hot, driving passion that would be thrilling and exciting one day, and full of arguments and missteps the next. I recall the many times this passionate, sexy man would sweep me off my feet, sometimes literally by whisking me up onto the kitchen countertop, for a deep passionate kiss. Other times out of the blue he would kiss my neck and whisper sweet things in my ear. Often times, while I lay on the bed, he would walk by, gather my feet into both hands and gently kiss them as he made his way through the room. This sweet man with his romantic side had my head and heart spinning in every direction.

We spent one weekend in the backyard with a fire pit, a blanket, and made love under the stars. We would spend hours talking about the things we had done, the hopes and dreams of things we desired to accomplish in the future. Stretched out onto a blanket with a warm fire at the perfect distance, our feet reached for each other while our hearts and minds would explore our pasts and discuss the future.

We could have easily become the dream team right there in Clarksburg, but along with the passion and excitement for each other, we dragged around with us vicious demons that were determined to destroy. Those early days we drank heavily, and marijuana was always on hand. Yet, just under the surface was another demon that had destroyed and robbed Ed of nearly everything good that he had ever accomplished in his 44 years on this earth. I wouldn't become fully aware of this sneaky demon until months later.

Those habits that I had developed in my previous marriage, were becoming deeper embedded in me, and I started using them to stabilize my existence. Then, in walks this gorgeous man who lavished me with all his affection and attention. This was just what this worn-out woman needed, a passionate affair with a handsome lover. Needless to say, I quickly fell head over heels in love.

Having already decided to ignore any red flags or warning signs, I plunged headlong into loving this man. I didn't bother to ask many questions but would spend hours listening. For anyone that has the pleasure of knowing my delightful husband, he can talk.... and talk.... and talk endlessly about any subject. I was so happy to have him in my life that I just listened. It was the perfect relationship, until it wasn't.

On those nights when I got a little too far into the bottle of rum or laid down too many beers, this destructive attitude would follow. I remember just before I was set to move to Savannah that the rum demon reared its ugly head one night. The next morning, I took the remaining part of that bottle to the kitchen sink and poured the lasts of its contents down the drain. I apologized to my sweet lover for allowing myself to get angry and out of control. The look on Ed's face as he turned the corner and saw me holding that bottle upside down over the sink was one of shock and possibly disappointment.

In our current existence it was a real waste of good liquor to be poured out like that. But I was acknowledging how my drinking was causing me to be someone I didn't like. I didn't want to be a sloppy, angry drunk. Yet there I was, rocking it like a pro.

Finally, the day rolled around and the U-Haul was packed, and we were set to move to Savannah. The plan was for me, my son, and our critters to go first, and a few weeks later I would return to West Virginia to gather up Ed and all his belongings and tools. Then we would start a new life together in a new city.

My Beautiful Savannah

THE MOVE TO Savannah came about through a weeklong vacation with my parents and my son in the spring of 2017. Ed and I were seeing each other, but his work would not allow him to join us. This was family time to get away and my first real vacation in about 7 years. In those 7 years since my last opportunity to enjoy life, my previous world and marriage had ended. With that came the loss of my farm and the selling of most all my horses. Several times I moved from West Virginia to Ohio, to Tennessee, to Kentucky and back to West Virginia. Usually all I had was an empty bank account, a broken-down car, and no social life which resulted in nights crying my drunk self to sleep. Those years were, by far, the worst years of my life. I knew I was ready for a change. I wanted a new place to start a new life away from the old funk that kept me stuck.

Now, feeling as if those ugly years were past me, I finally had a good job, money in the bank, and even paid leave for a vacation. But one thing remained, I didn't like where I was in life. I didn't' like Clarksburg and didn't really like my job. My son had finished high school early, so that no longer had a hold on keeping me in this place. I knew the day we left for vacation, I had set my mind on a move to a fresh new start that would bring this old girl back to life. This move would restore my heart and mind and cause me to begin dreaming again. Having something other than a little rental house and a mediocre job was what I needed to restart my life!

The minute we drove over that big, beautiful bridge that landed us in the heart of historic downtown Savannah, I knew I was home. I had lived in Savannah once before in my early 20's. I absolutely loved it, but my time there was too short and hindered by an abusive husband. That second arrival into this beautiful city renewed my thoughts and dreams of a new life. I knew without a shadow of a doubt that Savannah was where I wanted to be.

Mom and I spent much of our vacation time looking for housing and exploring the area. Prior to leaving Savannah, I had landed a job with Blue Green Vacations as a sales representative and secured a rental house. Upon returning to Clarksburg, I was thrilled to be able to give my two weeks' notice and quickly began making the plans to return to Savannah in three short weeks.

I had no problem packing that huge U-Haul truck and making all the necessary arrangements to make this move. My gypsy-like life, which consisted of more moves than even most military families, would bring one more move that was truly exciting for me.

At the age of 50 years old I was making a complete change to everything, new people, places, and things. My mom, who knew me best, suggested that this was an opportunity to reinvent myself.

Yes! That's exactly what I would do. I could create whatever kind of life I wanted. Having not experienced real happiness in life for several years, that's exactly what I would do. During the first three weeks of getting set up in this big house, I waited and waited for Ed to make the same commitment.

Would he really come to Savannah to start this new life with me? Would he have the same adventurous spirit as I did about a new beginning for his life–our life together? Was I wasting time waiting for him instead of getting on with my life, my plans, my new self which I could have easily created without a second thought? The day would finally arrive that would answer all those questions. Ed made his decision, gave his notice at work, packed up what remained of his life of destruction, and moved with me to Savannah.

We started our new life in a new city with new opportunities everywhere around us. All was NEW. However, one thing remained the same, "Everywhere you go, there you are!" I don't remember the first time I heard that statement. I don't remember the first time I used it. I do remember however the significance of that statement and the depths of its meaning within the first few months of our "new" life. Quickly, the booze, weed habits, and some other issues continued to surface. Arguing and ugliness was not how we wanted to treat each other. Then another problem came with the hard drugs.

Apparently crack cocaine was a whole new level of high that quickly grabbed ahold of my sweet man and turned him into someone who would rather hide in the bathroom with his phone and his drugs. Everything that took place in those months we will save for another time and place. For now, what will be shared is that an ultimatum was given. I told Ed to address this addiction, or we are done. I was not going to live this life. The last five years of my previous marriage was doused in drinking and snorting of pain pills. Turning a relatively fun, pleasurable man into a hateful angry ogre. I had already been down this road. Since I was not yet married to this man, now would be the time to bail out. Now would be the time to cut my losses and get back on track to a new ME! That is exactly what I needed to do. I needed to get on track for Donna, for my future.

On July 3rd, 2017, we made the decision to get sober and seek recovery from drugs and alcohol. We both made this decision. I was willing to dump my 4-to-5-year relationship with Mr. Bacardi if he was willing to end his relationship with the booze, drugs, and porn. This deal saved our lives. This agreement would take us immediately down the path of an outpatient treatment facility for Ed's drug addiction. Ed would spend all day in class, and we would work evenings as well as attend AA meetings.

It's sort of like repentance. We were walking in one direction one day, and we turned around and started heading in another direction the next.

This commitment to a new life was not easy to say the least. This required huge commitment of our time, efforts, resources, and desire to live a new way.

The first few days and weeks were hard. I had purchased tickets for a dinner cruise that would take us down the Savannah River for dinner. Then as the sun would set, we would watch the bright lights and explosive sounds of the fireworks display from the boat to celebrate our Independence Day. I had never really thought about it until that very moment, but we were experiencing our first little taste of freedom from the addiction that had us enslaved to sin and old habits. This first twenty-four hours into this new commitment was more like white knuckling it. We watched as most of the other partyers were staggering around with their mountainous fruity drinks. They were drunk with their fresh spirits flowing through their veins while we were in the very early stages of drying out. We were boiling on the outside from the heat and on the inside from lack of that which had kept us going over the last years of our life. This first Independence Day from drugs and drinking was more like a punishment and not much of a celebration. But we made it. We had to white-knuckle through that evening and every day since then. Thankfully, each day got easier after that first 24 hours of agony.

Ed would spend six weeks completing the out-patient rehab treatment program. This was not his first rehab; in fact, I don't know that he could tell you how many attempts at completing rehab he has done before. This one he managed to embrace in a new way. One of his favorite stories to tell is his first few days with his counselor, Ryan. Ryan told him that his years of addiction were selfish. Ed said it immediately angered him to his core so much that he wanted to come across the desk and split his face. I believe he told Ryan that was his first reaction. Ryan managed to get through to Ed in a way that no previous counselor had been able to do. They built a relationship on brutal honesty. Ed began to really implement these tools that were being taught during his 8 hours a day of treatment.

Day 1 of a new life of sobriety (Ed, Donna and Caleb my son)

Then we would either work the evening hours or attend an AA meeting. Many times, we would do both. For a solid 6 months we committed everything we had to this life of recovery. Living sober was our new job. It consumed us in every way, but truly that was required to become, and remain clean and sober.

Since we were new to Savannah, we had not made many friends. The AA teaching of "new people, places and things" was easy to do in a new city. There was, however, one couple next door who had started to come around the last few weeks, prior to our commitment to sobriety. Brad and Brandi were, for the lack of a better term, a hot mess. Both were in full blown addiction and hustling to keep up their lifestyle. They were on their way to being kicked out of their room in their shared apartment next door. They looked at our set up and thought, what a perfect place to land when kicked out of their current situation.

Brandi showed up just a few days into our new plan of sobriety, with the grand idea, of how she and Brad would be so helpful, should we sublet them the rooms upstairs. I didn't hesitate with my very clear, NO! But that would not stop her from continuing to come back several more times to poke and prod me into submission. Upon the third time she approached me on the subject, I took a step back and told her that I had been polite up to this point; however, she would now see my rude side. That was the last time she would enter my door. I also plastered my door with a sign that read "This is a drug and alcohol-FREE home". I recall relaying this story to the folks in the AA meetings. Referring to myself as a lion on the corner of my porch, daring anyone to come near what was mine and the lengths I would go to defend and protect what I found to be so valuable.

That is exactly how I felt towards this new way of life we had discovered. It was the most valuable thing that we could possess. We had clear, purposed minds, and our hearts began to long for something more. During the rough time when Ed was fighting against the drugs that had such a terrible hold on him, I would find myself standing over him in prayer for his mind, body, and spirit to be free from all this sin and addiction that had such a hold on him. Many times, while he slept, I prayed for God's help, not only for him but also for me to be strong and to know what to do. So, it's no surprise when he began to get clean and clear in his head and began to desire the things of God.

Church hurts were a part of my past. As a preacher's daughter and later in life, while serving in my own church, these hurts would happen. As if on cue, the devils' sly ways enticed me to quit attending church as do many other believers when "church hurts" enters the picture. Now, my soon-to-be husband wanted to attend church as a part of his sobriety program. I was somewhat resistant in this avenue, but because his needs were more important than harboring my old church hurts, we began the process of locating a church to attend.

The Need For Fellowship

THE FIRST ATTEMPT at finding a church was a total flop. Dead, dead.... DEAD!! You know I have to say, if you attend a dead church and expect new people to come and join in... WHY? Why would anyone want to be a part of something so dead that those attending don't even want to be there? In fact, most are only there out of a pure habit of getting up for over 40 years on a Sunday morning, getting in their cars, and making the same trip to arrive and park in the same spot. As if on cue, they stumble into the same location on the pew they have warmed for the same 40 years. For the love of God, get excited about what HE has done for you and live like you are truly in love with the One who has saved you from your sins and given you a new life.

Since that first place was certainly not what we were looking for, I began to ask a few people in our AA meetings. Ms. Jackie, who had become a dear friend, told us about her church she attended and invited us to meet her there that upcoming Sunday. Now this is what I am talking about! You could feel the energy from down the street, as the road was lined with cars attempting to find a place to park. Upon entering the huge wooden doors, the spirit of the Lord was present. The love of Jesus was on the faces of those kind, loving people who were quick to shake our hands and welcome us into their fellowship. We spent the next year at St. Paul CME church.

We attended the morning service, Wednesdays' Bible study and later began attending the Sunday School teaching. It was a great place to feed our hungry souls that were so empty and desperate to receive solid teaching and preaching. And the music was OFF the charts amazing!! Each service was full of true praise and worship, but I have to admit, it was the once-a-month men's choir that became my favorite.

The first few months we started going to St. Paul was the beginning of our life transformation. We would go and leave with tear-stained faces as the Lord would minister to our spirits in such a tangible way. I still possess the white lace trimmed handkerchief that Ms. Jackie lent to me on our first visit. I wept and wept at the reminder of God's great love for us. I did later attempt to return it to her, but she offered for me to keep it. I now use it as part of our communion service. It covered the bread that is used to represent the body of our Lord Jesus Christ.

Ed would be so blessed each week during service. There was such a freedom in worshipping. All could stand, sing, shout, and express the move of the Holy Spirit anyway one would see fit. The first week that Ed bolted to the altar and rededicated his life, they took him to the back and gave him some materials and prayed with him. The following week he hit the altar again. The third week the pastor said to him, "Son there is no condemnation in Christ." He recalled thinking I don't know what condemnation means. What was sending him to the altar every week was the guilt of the many years he had lived in the depths of sin. This huge wake of destruction was behind him, but he still felt that heaviness. When Ed began to really grasp this concept of what Pastor Thurmond meant that day, things began to change.

Understanding that once you have accepted the love of Jesus, once you have received the blessed gift of His transforming power of the blood He shed on the cross for YOU, all your sins are gone. There is no longer any guilt. Coming from a multiple offender, guilty of many crimes, this kind of freedom was life changing. I recall leaving church one afternoon, on the way home, I thought for certain Ed could just float home. He stated that he had never been so high as he was on the Holy Spirit.

"Feed People"

There came a time when we knew we needed to serve. Our time at St. Paul's was wonderful, but God made it clear this was our place to rejuvenate our souls; however, He had other things in mind when it came our turn to serve. It was at this time I went back to my roots. Having been raised the daughter of a Church of the Nazarene preacher, we investigated the local Nazarene church.

Upon arriving at the church that first Sunday morning, the crowd was much smaller and not near as vibrant as the crowd at St. Paul's. But that was to be expected as the diversity of the people was very different. Ed is easy to talk to and quickly makes friends. One sweet, slightly older gentleman would be the reason we returned the following week. Our dear friend Gary, with his kind smile and gentle eyes, would make his way to us to make certain we felt welcomed. He handed us a bulletin and gave us any other announcements that were upcoming. Most importantly he asked about "us." Who we were and what we did. Even more importantly, the following Sunday he was quick to follow up with where we left off the previous week. I can clearly state, had it not been for Gary, I am not sure we would have continued to return to the fellowship at the local Church of the Nazarene. His kindness made such a difference for us and can surely to be a lesson to all.

As time progressed, we became involved and attended Sunday school, Sunday evening and mid-week services. We were certain that we would develop some close relationships with several of the wonderful people in that body. Many folks began to share time with us outside of the regular scheduled events. These were the ones today that still hold a special place in our heart, and we feel as if we have a specific location in their hearts as well. Building such bonds and relationships are exactly what God had in mind for His Body of believers.

In that respect, there were others that were not easy to develop a meaningful relationship with. Some who would simply wave as they walked by us. A few even refused to acknowledge us all together, breezing right by us without so much as an attempt at making eye contact. They never had any thought or concern to find out whom we were or if we had accepted Jesus into our hearts and were born again.

Maybe they thought we were spies sent to check out how things were done in this church. Certainly, that was not the case, but how would one know if they wouldn't stop and make an introduction. Now the reality of this was that we were not the only ones with whom a wave and the nod of the head was all that was offered. This was how many were treated unless you were a member of a particular group. I shudder at this thought today as we minister to our own little body of believers. We are now the ones responsible for welcoming and loving new people when they walk in the door. We pray that all that enter our small church are embraced with a warm, inviting welcome.

Building a Business

ALL THE WHILE through recovery, getting married and attending church and meetings, we were building a business. The "dream team" in Clarksburg had ideas of creating a handyman service; Ed is brilliant with nearly every form of construction. I offered years of clerical experience as well as communication skills that together made us perfect for each other.

Immediately upon arriving in Savannah we put a listing in the local Craigslist that offered handyman services. Quickly, we began accepting work along this line. Ed is not afraid to take on any project even if it's something he has never done before. He will figure it out and give it a good ole college try. Early on when rehab was still required, our current job was in an empty home that demanded everything from a hole in the roof, drywall, plus painting inside and out. The beauty was, we could work when his new outpatient schedule would allow. We have found that God has this beautiful way of going before us and providing exactly what was needed during each step of recovery.

Our phone would ring often with new opportunities for additional work. Prior to leaving for an appointment, we would take it to the Lord. We would ask for His direction not only in providing the perfect clients but also providing us with the work and situations that was His will. Our every move was given and sifted through the hands of the Almighty. We began to receive calls from some influential clients which opened doors to other amazing jobs and wonderful clients.

A couple of our favorite clients were the owners of local restaurants. We first started providing simple tasks in their homes, such as hanging venetian blinds and small repairs. These tasks would lead to some of the most wonderful projects that were inside these old, glorious homes and rentals in downtown Savannah. Each project that was offered we took to the Lord for His guidance and His blessing. These moments of truly seeking His will for every aspect of our lives was a form of submission that was new to us, but we realized that previously we had made such a mess of things that giving it all to a higher power was a means of releasing our will to His. He blessed and blessed and even blessed us some more.

After completing many projects for this one client, we were asked to review a project, that by all accounts, scared the life out of my husband. The home was a glorious four-story home with side verandas on every level. From the bottom level there were two original beams that were rotting due to planters on the floor above. These planters had automatic waterers in them to keep these plants always looking gorgeous. In fact, every square inch of this five and a half million-dollar home was gorgeous. We became familiar with nearly every square inch of this home while working on the windows, patios, gazebos, shutters, walls, closets, and bathrooms in and around this historic home. All of this was because my incredibly talented husband had been entrusted to perform these repairs and maintenance. As a result, we were asked to replace these beams.

The time rolled around when the client was gone for a few weeks and his personal assistant and curator of the home wanted to have this project completed. Ed finally admits to me that he was a little afraid of this job. The technical difficulty in lifting the three levels of columns and porches to remove the existing beam that sat on a brick column had him rightfully intimidated. This was a job for a full crew of strong men, not a husband-and-wife team. But true to form, having spent some time in developing a plan in his mind, we set the date and agreed to do the job. I believe, without admitting it, the curator was a bit nervous as well, but to her credit she didn't say a word. However, I saw the slight concern on her face.

We had ordered the beams which were solid oak, approximately 10" by 12" and 7 feet long, from a local mill. These were massive to handle, but the first issue was to remove the existing beams while keeping the three levels of porch posts and floors secure. That morning we not only asked for the Lord's help but invited Him to join us for this wonderful project that required an extra hand.

Inviting the Master Carpenter to come to work that day was not just a symbolic invitation. Ed felt that Jesus himself had shown up that morning offering his wisdom and guidance for this difficult project. Five days later after long difficult hours, the beams were replaced, and all the painting completed. The side lights were reinstalled after they had been taken down for safety's sake. All three porches above were thoroughly inspected, and no stress or damage was visible on all three levels. Plus, now the lower level has been completed. Not one brick or area of plaster was hindered. Tackling this job was a major accomplishment for us, but it was also a wonderful reminder that our Lord was so very interested in every single aspect of our lives.

Jacks and lifts to elevate three porch floors

Job complete!

Through that client and the many projects completed in their personal home, rental properties, and restaurant, we were introduced to Steve and Mary, who would come to be our favorite clients. Steve and Mary had purchased a very large historic home on the corner of one of the busiest squares in all of Savannah. This home was an elegant Antebellum Greek Revival style home with nearly 10,000 square feet of living space. Two of our favorite projects we completed were for this client.

First, was a patio complete with pergola, flower boxes, and a built-in kitchen space including gas grill and a Green Egg. All this was custom built on site and perfectly suited to the space. This project was Mary's dream space. From inside the home, Mary could stand at her sink and envision the patio garden which would offer herbs for cooking, seating for entertaining and quiet morning with coffee and conversation. The original space had a battered pergola, worn-out walls, and a leak in the floor which happened to be the ceiling to the shop underneath. This project was not just a new pretty space, but also it had to solve a serious leak problem. We began researching and creating a plan to solve the leaks, but our main concern was how in the world we would get all this material onto this patio. Ed solved the leak problem by tracking all of the lines and reading some of the old blueprints from projects that had been completed with the previous owners. We created a lift from the street in order to get materials onto the patio roof and then used the same area for all the job-related debris. This was all about scheduling as the street was often very busy during prime day hours with the nearby hotel and shops.

Once a plan was in place, we began our work of removing all the old rubber roofing and striping and clearing anything that would hinder the elastomeric roofing material that would require three coats with ZERO rain in-between. From start to finish this stage of the project took twenty-one days, and in those twenty-one days we didn't get one drop of rain. Within hours of completing the project, the first rain in weeks came and proved that the system worked beautifully. This was completed in the late February to early March time frame, and anyone familiar with spring weather in Savannah can testify this was indeed a miracle.

We worked our tails off so that the clients could entertain their families coming for Easter. They would celebrate both Passover for Steve's family and then Easter for Mary's family. Mary was always the perfect hostess with exquisite taste and would pay special attention to every detail. We would return after the special Holidays and complete the remaining portions of the project by installing the kitchen section and final touches. This was a challenging project but extremely rewarding. I have no doubt that this space is still being used every single day, as every detail was perfected and well thought out.

Roof Patio in Savannah

Being pleased with that project, we began preparing for a complete remodel of Steve and Mary's master bathroom. Now this project would take us down to the bare bones of the room, by removing the 180-year-old wood flooring as well as portions of the plastered walls. This project was no small ordeal. We layered the antique staircase with protective paper and took every precaution to ensure nothing was damaged through the demo stage. The clients asked for our help in laying out the design for the room. I drew up two options and researched all cabinet materials. In the end we provided a custom rug designed marble floor that was perfectly centered between the shower, designer tub, and double sink.

On the other side of the room was the toilet and laundry closet. Much of the work and even some of the decisions were made while the customers were on their annual trip to Paris. Having worked with Steve and Mary for some time and understanding their needs and style, every decision was accepted and much appreciated. The only portion hired out was the large mirror and glass shower encasement.

When the pictures from this project reappear in our photo memories, they can't help but bring back a level of great accomplishment and pride that we were even offered these projects.

Master Bathroom

God poured out his blessing upon our business in the four years we worked in Savannah. Not every project was as glamorous or exciting as the ones mentioned. But each project we took, from the moment of committing our lives back into His capable hands, was GODS to bless. Indeed, He did bless and often we felt his protection from projects or clients that were not meant for us.

The Grey

The Grey

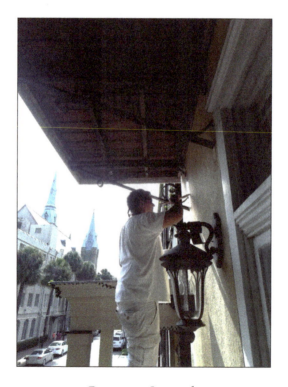

Downtown Savannah

Downtown Savannah

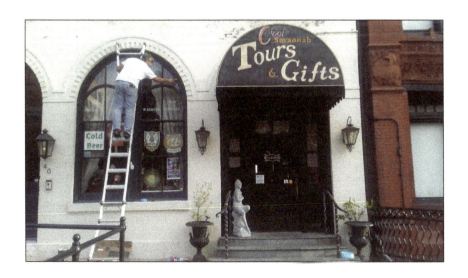

Part III
God's Calling Upon Our Lives

I heard the voice of the Lord, saying:
"Whom shall I send, and who will go for us?"
Then I said, "Here am I! Send me."
Isaiah 6:8

My Calling

I AM IN THE opinion that if you have a relationship with Jesus then you have a calling. A calling to live as the scriptures instruct and to bear fruit, such as love, joy, peace, longsuffering (another way of saying to be patient... yikes). However, for certain people there is a different calling. This calling requires more from your Christian walk with the Lord. I was sixteen years old and heard my dad preach a sermon on being called and asking the congregation about their willingness to do the Lord's work. "Here am I, send me" (Isaiah 6:8) was the passage of scripture I remember from the message that night. The next thing I remember is going to the altar and telling the Lord that if he was calling me into missions, I would be willing to go. I knew in my heart tht He was speaking to me that night through that message, through that lingering question of who would answer the question from the Lord.

Our church was always talking about missions. The church of the Nazarene was one of the only churches that boast being in more countries that any other denomination, other than the Catholic church. I gave a testimony that night that I had felt the Lord speak to me about becoming a missionary. I stood up before all those who were present and announced that I heard God speak to me about what He desired of me, a call into missions.

I finished high school and went on to a Nazarene college where I would begin my education. The only problem was that I had no real direction, no mentorship and no focus on what I wanted to do or how to get there. I felt like a wanderer, a gypsy in life. My life would drift from a variety of relationships, marriages, jobs, and hobbies for the next thirty years. At times I would focus on Jesus; other times I would not. I knew in my heart that He wanted my love, my attention, me! I also knew that I would never fully be happy without a relationship with Him, like the closeness and commitment I had experienced at times.

I wanted that closeness and bond with the Man who died on the cross for me. He alone would provide me with unexplainable peace. In the end my return to this wonderful Man would be through the love I have for another man, the man I would end up marrying. It would be Ed's desire to get to church and his desire for Christian fellowship that would get my feet headed back through the church doors and eventually lead me to the arms of my first love, my best friend, the lover of my soul, Jesus.

Through our path of recovery, we would soon find the clarity to seek God. That came quickly with step two in the AA meetings we were attending. "I came to believe that a power greater than myself could restore me to sanity." (step 2 of the 12 steps of Alcoholics Anonymous) I knew what that power was and had been familiar with Him before. He had befriended me many times and shown Himself to me in a variety of ways over the years. Once again, I fell at His feet asking for His forgiveness and mercy. So very quickly He lifted me into His mighty arms and showed me that His love was still there, always present. He hadn't gone anywhere but was simply waiting for me to turn back to Him. He began speaking to me again through scriptures, through my time alone with Him, and through reading the written Word of God. I so loved when He would speak to me, especially when he would give me special knowledge about certain things. I love His prophetic voice when He speaks.

My Calling

We were a few months into recovery when we started focusing on our relationship with the Lord. Devotions were an anticipated part of our morning. Ed had already read the "Jesus Calling" (a devotional book written by Sarah Young) for the day and was so excited to share with me what wonderful message was within that day's selection. As I stood in the bathroom preparing for our day, he stood in the doorway reading the devotion aloud to me. Soon he began to preach it. Without even so much as a thought, he was preaching this little segment within the pages of this little book. As if Jesus himself were standing right behind me, I heard a soft, sweet whisper in my ear...."Be prepared". I immediately knew what that meant. I knew I was being informed to prepare myself for what God was going to do through my husband. God wanted me to be ready for that renewed word which had been spoken deep into my husband's spirit those many years ago. You see I wasn't the only one who had stepped away from an old calling. I wasn't the only one who had wasted year, after year, living my own life and ignoring the call Jesus had in mind. Ed had been doing the same thing for nearly the last 10 years of his life too. God was revealing His call and His will for both of us in a way that only God can. And might I add, He did it in a way that would surely get our attention.

Ed's Calling

AS A YOUNG boy, Ed recalls often attending church with his mom and dad and on occasion with Grandma Pearl. There he has vivid memories of fiery, passionate preachers with vibrant speaking skills in sharing the Word of God. There were a few years his parents participated in church, but later, having fallen to the greatest scheme of the devil, they stopped attending. For the most part it was his younger years that he developed some knowledge of Jesus and what it is like, becoming a Christian. As a teenager and even into adulthood, there were sporadic moments where God was very present in his life.

There is a particular story that I always enjoyed hearing him share. It was during a time as a young married man with two young boys that he became interested in selling Amway. He and his wife would attend various seminars within a few hours' drive of their home. It was on their return trip from one of these events that Ed's youngest son would become very ill. That little man had a terribly high fever and broke into hives all over. Ed recalls stopping the van and getting onto the floorboard of that old van and praying for his young son. As he prayed, his son's fever broke; and he was immediately healed of what had attacked his little body. One minute he was lying out flat, and the next he was sitting up wondering what had even happened. A miracle took place when this man of faith prayed to his Heavenly Father and laid hands on his young son. Immediate healing took place that day. Even in the darkest dungeons of addiction, Ed would be reminded of the healing power of the name of Jesus.

I personally witnessed, several times, where my husband's faith and prayers would be immediately answered. We were nearing the end of our first summer in Savannah, Georgia. It was still terribly hot in the South because there are only a few months during the year that are not muggy. The A/C on my little car decided to quit. We were driving; and suddenly out of nowhere, a little puff of smoke came through the vent, and then there was nothing. No air at all was coming through these vents.

One thing is for certain, I am a heat weanie. I am a cold weanie too, but the super-hot, muggy weather in Savannah is unbearable without air conditioning. This happened on a Thursday. Ed reached out to his cousin who was an auto mechanic. They both did all they could think of to assess the reason for this thing to quit the way that it did. Sunday evening rolled around, and the decision was made. First thing Monday morning we would call a mechanic that specialized in auto air conditioning and hoped he would help us resume the comfort of proper cooling required for such a climate as our beautiful Savannah.

Making a quick trip to the store that Sunday evening Ed posed the question, "Have we prayed about this?" Well, the first thing I thought was, of course I prayed about it, however, the real question was, "Did I *really* pray about it?" Those prayers we throw in the air, hoping they find their proper receiving ground are not the real prayers, where we take our need or concern from the depths of our heart and through our mouths and lift them up by the Holy Spirit to the Lord's ear with every ounce

> Those prayers we throw in the air, hoping they find their proper receiving ground are not the real prayers, where we take our need or concern from the depths of our heart and through our mouths and lift them up by the Holy Spirit to the Lord's ear with every ounce of belief behind them.

of belief behind them. Without hesitation Ed began to pray. He spoke with boldness and belief and ended with an Amen. Without hesitation, immediately he reached down and turned the button to the right to the HIGH setting on the dash of the car. Cold air came streaming out of every open vent. We began thanking Jesus for answering our prayers, thanking Him for being the healer of the A/C unit on my Dodge Avenger, and praising Him for His amazing constant care for us.

That same car was stolen twice from the same location, and both times it was located and returned with barely a scratch. The first time was on a Saturday afternoon when we had just received a call to look at some work. I went to get changed, and Ed began loading the car with tools needed to do the work. He made the huge mistake of starting the car and running back inside for the drill batteries. Upon returning to the car, all Ed saw was an empty space along the street where the Avenger had sat just moments before. Coming back into the house he started yelling my name. He found me still in the bathroom preparing to leave. I have come to realize that when he calls me by my name, Donna, he has something really serious to tell me or he's not so pleased with me. Either way it is usually not good.

Quickly, I made three phone calls. The first one was to the police department; the second was to the insurance company to report the car stolen; and the last one was to my dad, since I have always known that he is a prayer warrior with a direct connection to our Heavenly Father. After answering the phone and understanding the urgency of the call my dad said "Sis, we will go to the one who knows exactly where your car is." Dad prayed that day for the return of the car and every single item that was in our car.

The following day after attending church and the special gathering afterwards, we headed home for our usual big meal, and then laid down for a nap. Barely asleep, I was suddenly awakened by a phone call from the police stating that they had located my car. The car had been taken for a joy ride and dumped just a few blocks away in the front of a church parking lot. There were a few scratches, and the front tire would later have to be replaced;

but everything else was just fine. Except… it was empty of gas! Apparently, the teens who had stolen the car for a joy ride picked up some friends and dumped all the tools in the back seat and trunk of the car.

The next day we began the process of assessing what was stolen so that we could make a report to the insurance company, hoping they would help replace some of the missing items. As Monday rolled around, we had to go back to work. That week the work was on the other side of town where we were making repairs on a nice lady's townhouse. It was late Thursday morning when the phone rang. The man on the phone was terribly hard to understand because he was yelling over the sound of a running lawn mower. After several attempts of trying to decipher what the man was saying, we began to believe he had knowledge of the tools that were taken from our car. Eventually, we were able to understand and found his location.

There was yet another church, just down the side street from where the car was found. The man, who had just called us, oversaw the maintenance for the church grounds and was taking care of the weekly mowing when he came across this huge hump of tools piled in the back area of the church. In that pile was also Ed's notebook that housed some business cards which gave this kind man a means to reach out and locate the owner to all these tools. We were tickled to death to go around the back of this church to load up all the missing tools that had been so needed those last four days. Once we got home, Ed assessed everything and found that one item was still missing. It was the million-dollar hammer. Early on I had discovered that every tool this man owned was "a million-dollar" tool, because he felt certain that each tool had helped him make a lot of money over its lifetime in his experienced carpenter's hand. He fully believed that the hammer had to be there, and we somehow missed it. We drove back over and scanned the area once again. To our surprise as we looked deeper into the higher grass just outside of the freshly mowed area, we found that precious hammer, that last item that completed dad's prayer in having the car and all its contents returned.

My car located in church parking lot

All contents from car located behind another church

These were just a few of the miracles we witnessed those first few months. These faith building moments helped Ed's faith and belief in God to flourish and develop. Each time God would deliver an answer to prayer or pour out His spirit upon us in a special way, our faith and reliance upon Him would skyrocket. God was doing a work in our lives on many different levels. We were seeking those things that God has spoken and planted in us over the years of our lives. In our walk with the Lord, there are times when we are totally centered on the Lord, and there are other times that we can be drawn away into the world which causes us to be distracted from God's ultimate plan. Ed and I were coming to a moment that many new Christians face. It is a moment where this newfound faith would be put to a potentially devastating test.

A Time of Testing

WE HAD BEEN in Savannah for nearly a year without a visit back home. We had recently gotten married, and many of our family came to support us on our wedding day. One guest was sorely missed, Ed's dad, Jack, who for health reasons was not able to make it to our wedding. Over the years there had been a lot of hurt and pain between these two men. This part of the story is not mine to tell so I won't even begin to attempt it. What I will share is what I witnessed for myself.

Early spring of 2018 a new movie came out that we knew we wanted to witness on the big screen. We scheduled our date night to our favorite restaurant, Sweet Potatoes, where we always enjoyed fantastic southern cooking. They are most famous for their banana pudding, but my personal favorite is the pecan crusted chicken and sweet potato fries. My mouth is watering at the thought of a plate arriving at my table with just a pat of melting honey butter in the center of the perfectly cooked chicken. However, I need to pull myself out of that dream and return to the importance of this story. We would only have to drive a short distance down the road to the cinemas for this special movie that would indirectly change our lives. As with any good movie, we were taken from laughter to tears easily as this story followed the true events of a father and son. So much of this story hit home with Ed and the relationship he had with his dad. At the end, as the credits began to roll, we remained quietly in our seats. As we wiped our eyes and noses with butter covered napkins from the bucket of popcorn, the only words spoken was Ed stating, "I need to see my dad".

We immediately made the arrangement with our work schedule to go back home to make our rounds and visit everyone. But this trip had a specific purpose. It was long past due that these two men, father and son, would forgive one another. We traveled early in May which also happened to be Ed's birthday. Having had some epic fishing a few weeks before, we brought with us some frozen whiting that I would fry for a fish dinner complete with all the sides. Everyone enjoyed this afternoon of a wonderful family gathering where the front porch was the best place to be on a spring day in rural West Virginia.

The week consisted of various family gatherings but most importantly Ed and Jack, father and son, just like old friends, would be able to spend quality time together. I didn't witness these special moments between these two men. But what I did witness, was the chains that had kept my husband bound up on so many occasions, began to fall away, freeing him from the years of hurt and pain. I believe Jack was able to experience the freedom of releasing past hurts and regrets as well. This visit, as we would find out three weeks later when Jack would suddenly breathe his last breath, was a beautiful gift from God. Believing that God is aware of our moment of conception as well as our last moment on this earth, I knew God had offered these two men the opportunity to remove the hurt and anger between them. A time of forgiveness, love, and affection would take the place of all those years of hurt and pain. This gift from God has been a moment that will forever change my husband. The reality of his own mortality at the loss of his dear dad has shaken him to his core.

It was a Monday afternoon when the phone rang, and it was his Momma on the other end telling me of this heartbreaking news. Ed was in the middle of a situation with Caleb when she called. My ears would receive the news first and would require me to share this news while I handed Ed the phone. I carefully watched my husband absorb this daunting fact. The pain and loss were not only felt by him but also by his mom. He wanted to immediately get in the car and head north to be near his family during this time of great sorrow. We would have done just that, but that morning we had started to work on a downtown B&B where we had just cut into two ceilings and found major water damage.

The owner had scheduled this week to be closed so that we could work. There was no option but to stay in Savannah. Complete this job prior to attending a funeral that would be scheduled for that coming Saturday.

Ed's eleven months of sobriety would be put to the test that week. In fact, he had experienced a small relapse just a few months prior, and this loss would be the ground on which success or failure would be established. As his wife, I offered him every form of support possible. I also convinced him, on one occasion, that he needed to verbalize this gut desire to get drunk or high because he really didn't want to ruin his current success. You see this is where the rubber meets the road, and this is where all things get more real. Anyone not having trod the path of addiction will never understand. It has been these times in his past, when the pain of life, pain of losing his boys, pain of ruined relationships, and pain of looking in the mirror and seeing all the destruction that his first response had caused that made this pain and suffering even greater. What a vicious and ruthless cycle.

This time we headed to a meeting. Our home group met on Mondays, and there Ed found comfort and care from fellow addicts who had faced similar trials and remained sober. Ms. Jackie, our Savannah angel, as we fondly refer to her, prayed over Ed asking our Higher Power, God Almighty, to provide comfort in such a time of grief. This time, being embraced and comforted by these friends with whom we had shared some of our darkest, ugliest moments during addiction, would now share in our grief, our pain. When those in AA use the phrase "sharing experience, strength and hope" this is what it looks like, crying with a brother, holding him, and praying with him. They would follow up in a few days with a phone call or text message to encourage continued sobriety.

I watched my husband work through every single gut-wrenching emotion that week. I witnessed his time in prayer and crying out to his Heavenly Father for comfort and wisdom. These next four days would create the solid rock foundation that Ed would return to many times as the place where he confirmed and established that commitment to God, as not only his Savior, but also his comfort and strength.

Activating the Call

WE PURCHASED OUR home in April of 2019. A small brick ranch that sat perfectly on a corner lot with a large fenced-in backyard. The property also came equipped with a large shop complete with power and shelving in the back yard. The dream team went to work and allowed 6 months to remodel and repair the home to be ready for the family to join us for Thanksgiving celebrations. My parents and my younger brother, Jon, and his soon to be bride, Jenny, would travel to Savannah for a full weekend of coastal fun.

Ed and dad went for the day out to Fort Pulaski to tour the area and location of where John Wesley would first step onto the Colonies. This was monumental. This day would prove to be another one of those moments where God would solidify His's call upon Ed's life.

Ed and Dad would share their calling stories as they drove towards the fort. Ed shared about a South African preacher that would come to the jails and preach and share the word of God. He preached one day about how the devil was like a roaring lion seeking whom he may devour. For wonderful emphasis this preacher shared how in the brush of Africa sleeping tents were caged off to keep the hungry lions from entering at night and devouring those who were sleeping in the wilds of the safari. He shared how one night he was awakened with a great need to go to the bathroom which happened to be located outside the caged sleeping tents. He rushed to the outhouse and returned quickly to the enclosure that was fenced for safety when suddenly as he shut the gate, a lion attacked, and the spittle from the lion's roar covered his terrified face. He had barely made it into the area of safety. But this event made for a great example of the scripture found in 1 Peter 5:8. When that story was shared in the jail, it brought Ed to his knees at that jailhouse altar, and he dedicated his life to Christ. Ed felt that God not only saved him that day but also stirred in him the desire to preach and share God's word with others.

Immediately, he gave up house (a term used for running items and gambling in jail) that day. Certain things became distasteful to him as a newborn Christian. He would read and study the word of God. Ed's time left on his sentence was 13 months. Within a month of Ed's salvation, he was miraculously released. Although he would sometimes stray from this experience and his call, the words were placed into his heart and would not be forgotten.

Ed shared this moment with dad that day and expressed that he felt he was called to preach. Dad, having been a preacher for many years and one to embrace others who sought to follow the call, gave clear instructions on how to get on that path of ministry. This included reaching out to our pastor and seeking a local preacher's license within the Church of the Nazarene. From that point he would need to go before the board and enter classes for education.

It was around this time at our church, that a Hispanic couple with a growing number of believers was seeking to use the church facility as a place to worship. They had been preaching from carport to carport to those who had been attending their services. With winter months approaching they presented our church leadership with a plan to share the facility. This couple came to our evening service one Sunday to offer their testimony and what God was doing through their willingness to serve.

It was during this wonderful testimony that I kept hearing them speak about how they do everything together. They told about how God used one to bless the other, and how their ministry worked because of the commitment of this husband-and-wife team. The Lord spoke so very clearly to me that night. He reminded me of my calling, not just to that 16-year-old teenage girl but to the wife of my husband. He showed me that we had done everything together and were the self-proclaimed "Dream Team". God wanted to work through each of us to perform His work. When we went to the pastor and later the church board, Ed and I shared our hearts' desire to serve and head down the path of ministerial studies, together!

Ed would begin this path as an Elder (preacher), and I would enter the path of a Deacon (service to the church). I would soon find out that there really was not much difference between the two. Outside of a few courses there are two major differences in being a Deacon or Elder. The elder would acknowledge a specific call to preach and be willing to go wherever the call would lead. This willingness to move was essential! The Lord knew I understood all about this part. My family had moved several times while growing up, and I knew that willingness to move was part of "the call". Clearly, I remembered this specific requirement that got my little mind thinking, "I am exactly where I want to be, my beautiful Savannah! I am not going anywhere…. And if God calls us away, surely it will at least be near Savannah so we can visit often." I almost wish I could take back those thoughts, those selfish thoughts of wanting what I want. God already had a plan in place, and He was in the process of working out every detail.

We scheduled a visit with our pastor and discussed the call God had on our lives. He invited us to attend the next board meeting where we would present to the board our testimony. When we finished giving our testimony, there wasn't a dry eye in the place (well maybe one). But our stories of how God has pursued us, all those years, and how we were now ready to submit and seek that which God desired for us caused the board to vote overwhelmingly to support our call and encourage us on every level. They even offered to pay for our courses of study. Immediately I started making phone calls to different schools so we could begin our ministerial studies and take on-line courses. I would end up choosing Mt. Vernon Nazarene University because

I had attended Mt. Vernon straight out of high school some thirty-three years previously. How ironic is that?

I did find myself, on several occasions, using the word "urgency." I felt there was great urgency in getting us prepared and trained for the work God had ordained. Possibly because we should have completed that call so many years earlier, or that our world was getting crazier by the minute and peoples need for Jesus has reached an all-time high. At this place in our journey, we are fully engaged in ministerial studies and living a wonderful life of work, church, friendships, and of course fishing! God had been preparing and orchestrating every detail so that we would be prepared for what was coming next. However, to get us fully lined up, there would be one more important lesson to be learned before the full plan would be exposed, a lesson in obedience!

A Lesson In Obedience

WE WERE NEARING the finish line for our second course in ministerial studies. COVID, that had hit the world and almost everything for a period of time, had finally come to a screeching halt. We were fortunate enough to continue to work on several projects at our church, and our on-line studies continued as usual. It was during these first few months of COVID that my little brother's wedding was cancelled due to the venues requirement to close. As you may recall, the concept was to close for a few weeks to "stop the spread". However, six weeks would pass before things started to begin to open. It was at this time that my brother and my mom would get together and decide a trip to the beach would be wonderful. Jon and his beautiful bride could get married there, and we could all join in on the festivities in Florida for a few days.

Most everyone jumped on board with the initial plans to head to Florida mid-May for a wedding and family vacation. The specific weekend was not the best choice for us, as that Saturday was our final class where we were required to attend via Zoom, turn in final papers and any other remaining details that would be due. But …. it was to be my brother's wedding so we would have to work hard to get things done prior to the date. Almost immediately I became unsettled about these plans. Within a few days the wedding portion was cancelled, as the bride's family was not yet comfortable travelling. So, our time on the beach would become a family vacation and a time to get together and relax. Certainly nothing wrong with that, but for some reason my gut was telling me this trip was not meant for us.

Have you ever created plans, got all the details in order, and even began to head down the road and somewhere along the way you stop and say, "Hey, wait a minute, I forgot something!" We had completely forgotten to FIRST go to God and ask him for His thoughts, His guidance, and His blessing. Instead, the conversation went something like this... "*Lord, will you catch up with me here and bless all these plans I've made without you. Lord, you know what I want, and I just want Your blessing.*" I know I am not the only one who has ever done such a thing. I just ran right ahead and then asked for God's blessing, asked for His provision in providing for these things I wanted, and asked for His protection for where I wanted to go. These plans were made only two weeks prior to the time we were to gather. In those two weeks I got more unsettled each and every day. The only time I could look back and recall feeling this uneasiness was when I took a horse to get bred. The breeding went wrong, and I had to bury a horse the following day. That same uneasy feeling that I felt while driving that horse to her breeding-gone-wrong appointment was the same feeling I felt when I planned to go on this family beach trip.

I made the mistake of expressing my uneasy feelings to my family the night before we were to meet in Alabama. Yes, I said Alabama!! Initially we were to gather in Florida, but Florida had not lifted some restrictions for certain travelers coming from other states. So now the trip had changed to Alabama, which was an additional two-hour drive time, and an extra five hundred dollars in expenses.

Clearly no one wanted to hear about my nausea and that I had not slept in days over this trip. In fact, I would be punished for saying anything for months following the trip. All I really knew, we were not to go on this trip. We still had the responsibilities for our classes, and the words from my oldest and dearest boss rang over and over in my head, "You do what you've got to do, to do what you want to do!" This trip was the opposite of this mantra.

Once we were packed and ready to go, and had the puppy sitter lined up, we started across town when we decided that it was a late start and would be better to start the next morning, bright and early. We got home, and I could clearly see my husband's disappointment. He had already scoped out the fishing and was very excited about a few days on the coast of Alabama as much as my other family members were. I was the only one with this anxiety about the trip. What was so wrong that I was feeling this way? Were we avoiding an accident by this clear stress upon my body, mind, and spirit?

This is what I do know. The very second, and I do mean the very second, that I placed the phone call to my sister that we would not be going, peace entered my body. Peace entered every core of my being. I made the announcement to everyone that we would not be joining them for this beach adventure. We would stay home and finish our class, write our papers, and do what we first set out to do.

PEACE!!! The Lord's peace is truly a gift. Having felt such anxiety one minute and complete and utter peace the next, I will never forget that the instant I obeyed, I felt peace. Unlike other times where the Lord speaks specific words to me, such as "be prepared "and "feed people", this time it was through my anxiety that He was telling me to do His will first and take care of His responsibilities first. Having made the announcement to everyone, including my husband, that we were not going, I went into the spare bedroom even though my husband was not happy with me and had the most restful sleep I had in days. The peace of my Heavenly Father rested upon me and allowed me sweet sleep. He knew how much I did not want to disappoint my family and my husband. Now He knew I placed Him and His will for me above all others. This moment of obedience and the peace that comes with being in His will is where I always want to be. I know what it feels like to be outside of His specific path for my life. I never want to feel that anxiety again because I did not, first, talk to Him about my plans. I don't want my plans; I want His plans for me no matter where they lead or what they might require of me to surrender. His perfect peace is all I need and desire. Anything less is troubling and no longer acceptable.

"For God is not the author of confusion but of peace, as in all the churches of the saints." 1 Corinthians 14:33

Having completed our class requirements, we took our own little vacation less than an hour down the coast of Georgia to St. Simmons and Jekyl Island. Two days of sightseeing and fishing gave us the rejuvenation we needed, and I was quickly out of the doghouse for not taking my husband to Alabama for fishing the Gulf coast. This short trip would allow us some time away and much conversation about what was next for us. Having finished two courses of study through Mt. Vernon Nazarene University and obtaining a local preacher's license, we signed up for the next classes in order that the following year we could be presented a district license before the district of Georgia. At least that was our plan.

I have always been a planner, one that looks ahead and sees what needs to be done to accomplish a certain goal. I remember calling some counselors to determine where we would take our next courses. During these discussions, I found myself saying the word "urgency". I felt there was no time to waste in getting ourselves trained and ready to serve. I had no idea

God would soon have us on the fast track and thrown into the deep end of ministry within the year.

We would complete our second project at our church before heading to West Virginia for the allotted time needed to repair Susie's bathroom. Several things happened before and during this second project that, for the lack of better words, dampened our spirits. First, I had already had the command to "Feed People" several months earlier. With all my excitement and ideas, the church leadership indicated they "wouldn't know how to facilitate that". Then during the weeks spent on the outside drainage project of our church, we were promised a key several times but were never given one.

Once we were told that the businesses that made keys were not considered "essential" because of COVID. Later, I found that excuse laughable as we were daily at Home Depot and Walmart where the key machines were always in use.

One morning we were scheduled to do some roofing repair, prior to fixing the ceiling in the teen room, where the obvious leak was causing mold growth. We started early that morning to beat the extreme mid-day sun of coastal Georgia in April. It was nearing 9 a.m. and the leadership was expected to arrive soon. I was in desperate need of a restroom. I messaged a leader to see when someone would be there to open, not only the restrooms, but also the rooms that stored some of our equipment. I was informed that he was running a little late. No worries, I can hold it. It was when the message came back that he was sitting in the long line at Dunkin Donuts for his mega sized coffee that I was past the point of waiting. Since things were still closed because of COVID, I hopped in the truck and drove home in order to relieve myself. I was really upset after being approved by the board to obtain a local preacher's license, having faithfully attended this church for well over a year, faithfully tithing our ten percent, helping complete one very large outside project, preparing to help with an inside project, but for some strange reason we could still not get a key. Ed was certain that during the process of getting our local license, that a background check was run and his lengthy, lifetime of run-ins with the law, was the cause for this continued delay in key privilege. After this very frustrating morning I went to the leadership, once again, and asked if there was a particular test that we still needed to pass in order to get a key. Yeah, I know my question was snarky, but I found it hurtful not only to my feelings but my bladder that can't wait lengthy times to be relieved. There were many other issues that often dampened our spirits almost every time we attended a service. However, God continued to tell us that this is where we needed to be, and we remained obedient.

The very next day after driving home to use the restroom, our friend Vincent, who occasionally worked for us, had car trouble and called us to help him. Ed recorded the location of where he had left his van, and we dropped what we were doing and went to lend a hand to our friend. As we turned off one road onto another road where Vincent's car was located, there on the left-hand side of the road was a church called "Keys to the Kingdom". Ed got the biggest kick out of this sign as we laughed and joked about this the rest of the way. It would become even funnier the following day when Ed and Vincent, while working on the roof and talking loudly over the music below, discussed this church called the "Keys to the Kingdom". Both Ed and Vincent rejoiced that Jesus is our Key to the Kingdom, and were so thankful to be His friend. It was at this very moment Ed turned around, and there stood the man with the much-anticipated KEY to the church. And wouldn't you know it, he had it made at Walmart.

There were many spirit dampening events that transpired during our time at this church. The truth is, not everyone is going to support you in what God has called you to do. How could God possibly use this old drug addict with fading jail tattoos on each arm? Not everyone is going to agree that God has called us into ministry and that He does have a specific plan that only we can fill. I am thankful for such moments that strengthen our faith and our trust in God Almighty and that my salvation does not depend on what others think of me or my husband. How God sees us is more important than how I am viewed by anyone else.

Now we had finished our final project and were ready for our next assignment, to work on Susie's bathroom in West Virginia. God had commanded me to "Feed People". Later He gave me a dream about a little country church where the rapture would take place and nothing but little piles of dust would remain. We had started our third course of study, while we traveled and now anticipated a wonderful time away while doing a job for Ed's mom. Additionally, I now understand that deep, settled peace only comes when walking in perfect obedient to His will, not our own. We could never have known that this working vacation would forever change the course of our lives. Eagerly we loaded the truck with tools and our dog and headed north for a month in West Virginia.

Part IV
Help Wanted:
The Dream Team is needed in West Virginia

"Brothers, I do not consider myself yet to have laid hold of it. But one thing I do: Forgetting what is behind and straining towards what is ahead"
Philippians 3:13

Heading Back To Savannah

IT WOULD TAKE us three weeks to complete Susie's bathroom; and in that time, we had several discussions with Happy Herman (That was the way he introduced himself, and it suited him perfectly). We knew it was our calling to restore this old church, to make it useful again. Happy Herman had ideas and plans, but his age and distance from the church would make developing those plans difficult. We all agreed that God had organized that fateful meeting that Wednesday morning, and that God wanted our hands to be given the task of repairing the old church.

Everyone continued in obedience to the Lord's plan to restore Spruce Grove Church. Without hesitation Happy Hermon handed us the keys to the church. He entrusted these two fellow believers, passionate for our God and King, to follow His leading and restore this little ole church in the valley for His service, for His will, for His magnificence.

With a prospective plan in place, we went back to our beautiful Savannah, Georgia. Immediately, we made a lunch date with several couples with whom we trusted to share our news and give us sound Biblical advice, or slap us upside the head if need be. Every single one agreed we were following the Lord's will. I will have to admit my dear friend Arlene was not happy with me. She said very little during the lunch meeting and even afterwards. With her gentle way, she was expressing how she would miss us if we did not return to Savannah, after the repairs on the old church. Somehow, she knew God was taking us away from their fellowship and delivering us to another location to serve.

Our hearts were elated with this new adventure yet saddened as well. God had provided us with real, genuine friendships with these two wonderful, Godly couples. Buddy & Dianne and Gary & Arlene would send us on with love and a mountain of continuous prayers towards the mission God had prepared for us.

*"The way of a fool is right in his own eyes;
But he who heeds councils is wise." Proverbs 12:15*

During our two weeks stay in Savannah, there were a few loose ends that needed to be completed. There were little jobs and conversations with folks to let them know that we would not be available to consider their projects at this time. Although we probably knew in the back of our minds this was a long-term move, we weren't really expressing it that way. We wanted to keep this door open for God to show us what was next. All we really knew was God wanted Spruce Grove church repaired for His work, and we were the ones called for the job. I was told to feed people, and my husband had a fire in his belly to preach the Word of God.

With those two things in mind, we moved forward with Gods plan. We purchased a little twelve-foot cargo trailer during this time in Savannah. This would be the means of transporting all of our tools and essentials back to West Virginia where we would live for the next few months. Just before all this happened, we had completed a full remodel on an apartment where the customer replaced all appliances. We retained the refrigerator which worked but had an occasional noise and missing a bottom produce drawer.

That old refrigerator was packed along with our fairly new Puffy mattress, tools, clothing, and pets to head back to Braxton County, West Virginia.

Let the Work Begin - August 1, 2020

IMMEDIATELY I STARTED the process of filling out all the paperwork for a nonprofit so that I could purchase through Mountaineer Food Bank in order to start a food pantry. My husband began the long tedious task of getting up under that old building and addressing the many issues that would require repairs. Thick mold from previous flooding and no vapor barrier had caused major damage.

Water line breaks and rotten floor joist were just a few of the problems that existed after years of neglect. Many times we thought that this building was too far gone, past the point of usefulness. However, we would be reminded of God's call, His way of making things work when we could do nothing.

We would arrive on August 1, 2020, to begin the work. Upon arriving and assessing the damage, we made a plan as to where to begin. Many times, the thought that we had bitten off more that we could chew would creep into our minds. There was so much work that needed to be done from the front of the building to the back and all up underneath. Everywhere was a monumental mess that stared us right in the face, but we trudged onward.

Day two began and I heard from my dear friends Lonnie and Betty Fast from Fairmont. They had been camping and had reached out hoping that we were available for them to stop in for a visit. I looked around and said, "Why not!" There was no cleaning up for visitors. Why not let them see what we had gotten ourselves into. I had not seen Lonnie and Betty since leaving West Virginia in April of 2017. They had yet to meet my husband but had heard so much about him and about this church. I am sure their curiosity about our plans, the dream and the church had them wanting to hear all about how this had transpired, directly from the source.

I greeted them at the side door and led them around all the areas of floor that were unsafe on which to walk. As I escorted my guests to the kitchen area, having already been through the worst parts, I recalled Betty looking around and repeating "Oh my.... Oh my" repeatedly. I am sure she thought we had completely lost our minds. How would this dilapidated, decaying building ever become useful again? Without running water there was little we could do to clean up at this point. The place was really disgusting, and I could see their concern that we had lost our marbles while living in Savannah.

Betty went back to their camper and pulled out some homemade West Virginia pepperoni rolls and hotdog sauce for lunch that day along with a half a gallon mason jar of sweet tea. The microwave was the only thing in the kitchen in working order. As she warmed up her picnic lunch, I filled some plastic cups, and we sat around a plastic table and chairs to share a meal and the story that had brought us to this little country church in rural Braxton County.

It was now our opportunity to tell them how this all came about. I took them back to the dream and shared with them the very unusual meeting with Happy Herman who would take us to this church, exactly as I had seen in my dream. I even shared the story of my lesson in obedience. With laughter and some tears, we laid out our story, and as they listened they began to understand. This was not some whimsical fantasy but GOD at work! These dear friends of mine, whom God placed in my life over 25 years ago, had offered me solid Christian advice many, many times over the years. I valued them greatly, and over traditional pepperoni rolls and sauce, I shared every bit of our story that had brought us back to West Virginia. It was clear to them that God was doing a work, and these doors that had been opened were done so by His hands.

"These things says He who is holy, He who is true. He who has the key of David, He who opens and no one shuts, and shuts and no one opens"
Revelations 3:7

Avoiding those areas of rotten floors, we ended our visit in the sanctuary. Lonnie prayed over us and mentioned the many prayers that had been prayed at the altar over the years. There were times of fellowship, salvation, healings, and all the works of the Lord over a lifetime in this old church building. It's likely that Lonnie and Betty's conversation on the way home that day was one which included the need to pray for these two kids who are following the call God had on their lives. It wouldn't be long before our energy and effort would be tested. But God not only sent us to this little broken down country church, but He also provided us with prayer warriors that would be lifting us up in prayer every step of the way.

It would take us nearly five months of work to repair the church to some form of working order. Our first task was to make the back portion of the building, previously the Sunday school room which doubled as a fellowship space, into an apartment where we could live while making the needed repairs. We had taken all our savings and later the proceeds from our house sale in Savannah to afford to make these repairs. We also put ourselves on a tight budget since we were no longer working as we had in Savannah and put all our efforts and money into the rehab of the church and getting this ministry off the ground.

The needed repairs to this old building were much more advanced and disgusting than we had recalled from our first assessment. There was thick white mold that covered every single inch under the back portion of the building. The water lines had burst at some point, spraying for hours the floor joist and subfloor.

Later, we heard that at least twice, flood waters rose just below the main subfloor of the church. This church sat in a valley with a wall of stacked rock and oak trees that supported a county road on one side. Then on the other side was a dirt road that brought everyone down into the valley to this church and on past it to a few neighbors on Spruce Grove Road. Along the dirt road was a creek that was mostly dry, except during heavy rains. Also, at the back of the church was a creek that ran year-round.

This creek would get pretty low during dry times but could swell over the banks during heavy rains. During one heavy rain, Ed was out with his chainsaw cutting a tree that had come down from further up the creek but had made its way to the little bridge. It was causing quite the dam, backing up lots of debris and causing the water level to rise even higher.

It's in these moments I have a higher appreciation for men being men. Bravely, Ed would stand at the edge of this bridge with a fired-up chainsaw and carefully cut away branches and even somewhat systematically demo this tree so that the debris could once again flow freely. This one tree could have caused so much more damage, possibly even taking out the bridge, had it not been for the brave, willing hands of my husband. In the pouring down rain, I stood along the bank with my phone so I could record this event or even call in back up should that be needed as well. Either way I was useless.

Log jam at the bridge – my brave man

Nearly flooding the church – Summer 2021

Let the Work Begin - August 1, 2020

Removing the mold and repairing the water lines would be the first of our priorities. That first week my dedicated husband would crawl up from under that mess and come out wet, muddy and wanting to quit. But as soon as he would reach the fresh air and feel the sun hitting his face, a new friend would be there to inquire, "What are you doing here?" The first time this happened was when an old man by the name of Laco Mace appeared. There he stood with his hands on his hips and looked Ed square in the eyes and said, "What are you doing here?" There is nothing like getting right to the point. This first visitor would be just the encouragement Ed would need.

Ed learned, as Laco shared his stories about this country church, that this man had taught Sunday School at Spruce Grove Methodist Church for over 25 years. Also, Laco had attended the little school that had sat at the back end of the property line. Just before we had discovered this little church, the local fire department had performed a controlled burn on the old school building as part of their training. This sweet man would talk about his moving to Ohio as a boy when no work was available around the area.

It was either move or starve to death. This area has seen tough times in the past. Laco, showing up that first time and sharing with Ed all his memories of this old building, was just enough encouragement to get Ed through a few more days dealing with the major mess we had taken on. Laco would become a regular visitor for the first few months. Every couple of days or at least once a week he would stop in to check on Ed's progress. Laco's mind would repeat the same story over and over again. Each time he spoke about teaching Sunday School, he would weep and get emotional about his fellowship with his friends that had once attended here as well. Many good times and lots of love were shared over the years in this old church.

"Feed People"

We were able to move into the apartment portion within a few weeks. Having running water and bathroom facilities was finally checked off the list and allowed us to set up house in the little space in the back. It would be our first meal cooked and eaten when our second visitor would arrive. Ed had worked hard that day, just showered, and laid down to rest and pray while I prepared dinner. I was grilling chicken in the back when I looked over to see a young man sitting on the bridge. I went inside and told Ed that a young man was outside by the bridge and might be someone who would be willing and able to help with the work. Ed had been praying that if it *be the Lord will* He would send him some help because he couldn't do this work by himself. Immediately, Ed went straight over to see him and struck up a conversation with him. Within just a few minutes they both began to walk back to our apartment. Ed had invited Will to dinner. Yes, I said his name was Will, and yes, Will would be available to go to work the very next day. What was even more helpful was that Will was a small, thin little fella. He would be able to shimmy up under those tighter areas under the building. We praised the Lord that it was His will in sending Will along to help.

Selling Our Savannah Home

TWO MONTHS WOULD pass as we put all our effort, time, and money into restoring this old church. We had continued paying the bills on our home in Savannah and several times discussed selling our little ranch that sat on the corner lot in our quiet neighborhood. We debated about options, but I recalled a conversation that I had with a lady with TMCI (The Missionary Church International). This was the organization that provided us with ordination papers and means to operate our ministry. She had told me how she and her husband sold their home so that when a difficulty arose months later, the option to run back was no longer there. They had fully committed to the plan God had shown them.

It was time for us to make that same commitment. We knew in our heart that this was where God had planting us for a work of ministry, not just repairing the church but making this old church building a place where God would use us to fulfill an even greater plan. Ed was more resistant in this process than I was, I was ready to sell and commit completely to being in Frametown. This seemed backwards because this was Ed's hometown, and I was the new kid in a close-knit community. We decided we would list the property for sale by owner and see if there was any interest. The only interest it gained was from a local realtor who asked us to list the property with him. We agreed. We listed the home for what we thought was much more than its value based on the per square foot price for neighboring properties. Without boring you with all the details, we received an offer within 48 hours for five thousand more than our asking price. The sale went through without a hitch! In my experience of purchasing properties (not extensive) this was the easiest and most fluid of any sale.

There is an essential element from February earlier that year. We had attempted to refinance the property through our local bank. We had purchased in a non-conventional way similar to a land contract. During this process we just had the appraiser give the bank his appraisal when the bank decided they couldn't do the loan. We never did see the initial figures by that appraiser done in February. I was so frustrated about this process. I pouted around for a few days on how the bank mishandled the deal, how the loan officer had lied. On and on feeling really mistreated, I finally got over it and moved on.

Eight months later, in October, we listed the property for at least thirty-five thousand more than what we fully expected the property to appraise. Once again, our amazing God had gone before us in preventing a much lower appraisal to have been assessed and now allowing us to sell the property for a greater rate of increase then the entire area around our home was experiencing. This is a great lesson for us all. When one feels a door has clearly closed in your face, consider that God has gone before you and already knows what is happening. Many times, He is looking out for our best interest, but our willful, stubborn, and at times, rather selfish nature gets in the way. Praise the Lord for His foresight.

When we agreed with the realtor to list the property, we managed all details long distance up until the point of final closing. This closing would require going to our dear neighbor Joan and getting the spare key. Ms. Joan was our sweet Christian neighbor who provided close watch and care over our home in Savannah while we were gone. She watered my plants and ensured nothing was amiss during our months in West Virginia. The realtor would also do a full walk through and note anything that might require attention. He did suggest someone come in and do a thorough cleaning for showing. Although we had left the home in decent order, a deep cleaning was needed and helped ensure a quick offer.

After all was agreed upon the closing date was just around the corner, Susie drove us to Savannah so that we could leave the truck in West Virginia and return with a U-Haul and my car in tow. Vividly, we remember our arrival at our pretty little home in Savannah. We pulled into the driveway with the yard perfectly manicured because we had kept up the yard service while gone. Upon entering our home Susie said, "Are you kids sure you're doing the right thing? This is such a lovely home". My immediate reply was "We are working towards our eternal home". I will have to admit that walking into our beautiful home with all our personal touches in every room and our belongings set about that had been established between two hard working, determined people was not easy; but it was not something we would hold onto. God's dream for us would drive us forward to see what would lay ahead and where God was taking us in this new journey. God clearly had a plan for us in this new adventure that He was leading. We certainly didn't understand everything He was doing, but looking around at this home that God had blessed us with; within a few short years of giving Him our all, we wondered what more could God do with that little church in the valley?

We would use our time to pack, visit friends, our church, and even eat at our favorite restaurant for that yummy pecan crusted chicken and sweet potato fries. The day would arrive where we would sign the final papers to sell our home, turn over the keys, and hug our dear neighbor Ms. Joan. Loading our automobile into the car hauler, we would make that final trip over the Talmadge Bridge that led out of Savannah. This time there we no tears but great anticipation for what awaited us back "home", our puppy Molly Moo, my parents who lived a half hour away, Ed's mom, 10 minutes away, and a growing passion to stay saturated in the peace of being in complete obedience to our Heavenly Father.

Memories of our life in Savannah

Arriving to our "Under Contract" house (Susie and Ed)

A walk along River Street

Tybee Pier – favorite fishing spot

Deep sea fishing trip for Ed's birthday

One of the many times on the pier

"Feed People" - Opening a Food Pantry

MIRACULOUSLY MY APPLICATION for a nonprofit went through quickly. Everyone that I spoke to about this was floored that it happened so easily. I believe it was the hand of God at work preparing me for the work He had designed for us to do. December 1, 2020, would be the opening day for our food pantry; that was 4 months from the first day we arrived to work. I had purchased some items from the food bank, Sam's Club, and even Walmart to stock my newly built shelves. Ed had obtained some rough-cut lumber from his cousin who runs his own lumber mill and gathered enough boards to put together two sturdy sections of shelves. We also went to Lowes and purchased a refrigerator / freezer, one of those appliances that would switch between freezer and fridge depending on the current need.

I had set up a rather heavy schedule of providing meals for every other Friday or Saturday. Fridays would be a lunch meal and Saturdays a breakfast. My mom traveled from Summersville to help me prepare the food and packaging. We offered these meals as a pilot program to see what interest there was or how great the need was in our area. In the end there wasn't a great interest. COVID kept people behind closed doors; and since this idea was geared towards the senior or elderly population, they weren't keen on accepting our offer of meals.

Shortly into our program I received a phone call from friends from a few counties north of us. Lonnie Fast called me with details about the World Vision Appalachian Project and the food boxes they were offering. The following day I made a few phone calls and found out that since we were a nonprofit organization in the state, we could obtain a pallet of these "farm to family" boxes. We immediately made the connection and set a time and date to pick up these boxes of fresh food. These boxes contained milk, cheese, chicken nuggets, potatoes, onions, and yogurt. What a wonderful blessing to be able to distribute these boxes to our community just weeks before Christmas.

Since we had just opened our pantry, we were not well known in the area and ended up delivering many of these boxes around the community in a random manner. We didn't have the refrigeration space to keep all the food at the proper temperature; however, with it being winter, the cold of the trailer allowed us some time to get things distributed. My husband and I set out throughout the immediate vicinity and delivered "farm to family" boxes. The look on people's faces was priceless. How often do you have someone show up in your driveway or front door with a box of wonderful fresh food just before the Holidays when many are struggling to provide for their families? These boxes of food were received with open arms and grateful hearts.

One of our boxes would go to our dear neighbor and old Spruce Grove friend, Ms. Arabelle Long. Arabelle had spent her lifetime serving her neighborhood church. We visited her one evening to bring a box of "farm to family" food and were greeted by her caregiver at the side entrance to her farmhouse which sat beautifully in the valley. We introduced ourselves as the new pastors at Spruce Grove, although at that time we hadn't officially opened the church.

Ms. Arabelle was a delight. She sat upright in the comfort of her bed while we shared all the news about reopening her beloved church. She listened for the longest time nodding and smiling and would later admit she struggled to hear all that we had said. She asked if we would sing for her, and of course we did. We were out of tune and a little squeaky, but she was delighted to have her visitors sharing and singing for her. I could tell this lovely lady must have been a visionary in her lifetime as she still had a vision for her beloved church in the valley. She spoke of things she could visualize as possibilities for the building that had closed several years ago. With light in her eyes, she spoke of how it would make for a lovely wedding chapel. I certainly agreed. The little church was adorable and would make for a perfect setting for any wedding couple. It was her next suggestion that described this sweet lady to a tee. She believed that the church would be a wonderful place to offer painting class to the neighborhood children. I later discovered that our gentle, new friend was an artist herself with a passion for others to experience the joy of painting. This would be our one and only visit with Ms. Arabelle. Shortly after our visit she would be moved to Flatwoods to be cared for by her son and not long after would go on to meet her Heavenly Father. I will always remember our visit with this kind lady.

As time would go on and I would meet others who cherished this old church, everyone always spoke in the most loving way of my new friend Arabelle. She was a true lady who was generous to her family and church.

Another element to our meeting with our neighbor, Arabelle, would be to receive a phone call early the next day from another woman who had grown up in this same adorable church. As her luck would have it, she had just gotten engaged to a kind sweet man. In sharing the news with her sister, she commented on how she had always wanted to be married in Spruce Grove Church. Her sister was delighted to inform her of the new life being breathed into this old, yet not fully forgotten, church. She was quick to track down Ed's number and without hesitation called. It was just as Ms. Arabelle had desired. Spruce Grove's bell would once again ring out through the valley announcing the couple's nuptials. Mike and Lori would be married just one week prior to Easter, spring of 2021. We had Spruce Grove all dolled up for their special day where the family, who were raised within the walls of this precious building, would celebrate their baby sister's wedding day. This sister would be marrying the man who would promise to love her till death do they part. We attended as special guests of the couple, even though we did not know them personally. Having followed God's call, this special building was now available to fulfill the desires of one beautiful bride's heart. I continue to be in awe of the plans and purposes God has in store for this church. This certainly would not be the end to the many fulfilling moments in Spruce Grove Church.

December 13, 2020 would be our opening day for Spruce Grove Community Church. We were so thankful to all our friends and family who came out to support our first service. During the first few months we had a few faithful attendees that would show up every week, weather permitting. I would attempt to lead a few songs in worship, but with my alto voice, I would often screech my way through or bring the key down so low that no one else was comfortable with the melody. Also, my husband would begin putting together weekly sermons that caused us to spend more time digging into the Word of God. We clearly understood that this is what God had intended for us to be doing all along.

It was about mid-February when we would experience our ultimate low. It was a cold, winter Sunday, and only two people attended our service that day. A young couple who lived over the hill from us came to church that Sunday. This was a couple that Ed was determined to see recover from addiction. They came a little early so I offered them the use of our laundry room to wash and dry their clothes. They were living in a converted shed with no running water or electricity. A little creek in the back of their shed provided them with water for their cooking and immediate needs, but traveling to Sutton or funds to wash clothes were not available. I had no problem offering them the use of my new mix-matched washer and dryer we had picked up from the scratch and dent aisle at Lowe's. In the rehab of our little apartment, the area that used to house a small men and women's restroom was now opened up for a combined bathroom / laundry area. Ed skillfully remodeled the olds women's' bathroom into a laundry room, and the old men's bathroom into a shower area. We had everything we needed in our little apartment in the back of the church, and on that particular Sunday we offered what we had to this young couple.

Come 2pm, they would be the only ones in the service that day. I am certain that if their clothes had not been in the dryer, they would have probably headed to their car and went home. But we went on as if the place was full. We did our announcements, sang a song, and Ed preached his heart out. This provided us with an opportunity to minister a few more times to this young couple.

After that Sunday they came to the pantry, and shamefully, I must admit that my greatest failure was with this young couple. They arrived one day without notice and not on a regular pantry day. Initially, I hadn't heard them since I was in the back rooms of the apartment. When I did go to the door the young man commented that I must have been in bed, or something of that nature. I really don't remember what I said to him, but it was short and abrupt. I hadn't had a chance to put on a sweater, and I was frustrated and lashed out at him. Then I went back into the apartment and got my jacket. By the time I got back into the pantry, I saw them load into their car and proceed out of the driveway.

I was so ashamed and mortified that I had allowed myself to snap at this young man. I told my husband what I had done and proceeded to put a box of food together. His only words were," What are you doing?" My reply was, "I have to try to make this right and apologize". My husband never whispered another word to me, never lectured me on my bad behavior. He knew I felt horribly ashamed of my actions. We put together a box of food, loaded it into the car, and then we headed to their humble home along the edge of the road. This was my first time visiting their home. Ed had been there once before and knew exactly where they were living. As we pulled off the edge of the road across from their little home, I noticed step stones and yard trinkets around the front of their property.

They were attempting to make a home out of this meager shed. The young lady met me at the car as I poured out my apology to her and asked if I could speak to her boyfriend. She indicated he was to hurt to speak with me, which made me feel all the more ashamed. Having done all that I could to right this terrible wrong, I slid myself back into my car for a quiet ride home.

I made a decision that day that I would never, never, never allow myself to pop off with this kind of ugliness ever again. I would always do my very best to consider how the other person might feel before anything exits my mouth, especially when it comes to those we serve. This couple would soon break up because the young lady tired of living so meagerly. The young man would struggle keeping a job and would soon move back to his hometown. There he found some stability, work, and even began going to a church. The last Ed heard from him, he was now a member of the local fire department, had a new girlfriend, and was a regular at his church. This young man was now clean, sober, and stable. I am thankful to be able to report his success. I know I failed him terribly, but God never fails. Never does God let go or give up on someone. He always looks at them and sees that delightful person He intended them to be from their conception. I praise His Holy Name for His greatness.

Spruce Grove Community Church Opens

Spruce Grove Church would start rather meagerly with a handful of regular attendees for the first 6 months. My energy and ideas on how to serve our community would flow seamlessly from concept to creation in my head. Finally, the time would come to put all my thoughts together and gather the necessities needed to pull off all my ideas. The first big event would be to have a VBS for the children in our area. We began planning with a handful of committed individuals to kick off our very first Vacation Bible School for the end of May 2021. My sister-in-law would loan us their program that their church had used a few years back. As luck would have it, this was the same program that my mom had used at her church, and she was very familiar with the theme and music which was invaluable.

What would transpire over the few short months of planning VBS would provide me, a new transplant to this area of Braxton County, great inspiration. People we had met through other churches or neighbors would immediately volunteer their time, efforts, and talents just as a need would arise. I cannot express how miraculously this happened. Two ladies from our fellowship at Shiloh agreed to lead the music portion of our program. Lisa, who is the mother of nine children and doesn't look a day over twenty-eight, brought to the table the talent and energy needed to lead every single fast-paced song on our playlist. Even keeping up with the most energetic of our young children, she rocked it in a way that only she could. By her side was Bethany who was a tremendous support in various areas. Our friend Dani Ramsey would be our teacher for the week. She took the material, devoured it, and each day delivered a custom teaching suitable for her students. The final day she would present her teaching to the entire class. Without question her delivery had everyone, from the youngest of four to the oldest of seventy-eight, mesmerized with the plan of salvation. At the end of her presentation, nearly every child hit their knees ready to pray and accept this amazing Jesus that had been taught so expertly at each child's level. Throughout the week, each worker would offer these little ones the love of Jesus, and each child hungrily received.

Our first event was a super success. We had twenty-five children by the end of the week. Many of those children along with their parents attended the presentation on Sunday. The support from the community was something that will forever impress me. I know it's a God thing, but this is also a Frametown community thing. This is how they support and care for one another. As I write, I am nearing three years of being a part of this community; and I am still, at times, pleasantly surprised how these men and women work and care for each other. As I mentioned earlier, I am somewhat of a gypsy. I have floated here and there over my lifetime, and because of that, I have never really felt a part of a community like this. I am so thankful that the Lord brought me to this rural part of West Virginia for many reasons, one of which is being able to witness and be a part of such a circle of friends and neighbors, this beautiful thing called community.

Our little, growing group pride ourselves on being a church that prays! Each week we distribute prayer sheets that are full of the needs of the community. We are seeing lives changed and things happening because of the prayers of the faithful.

As we got started in offering worship services, I would lead the singing and present the announcements, Ed would lead in prayer and preaching. I have a strong alto voice and am fairly good at harmony. What I am not so good at is leading the congregation singing. With my low voice I would struggle getting the song started off low enough so that when arriving at the higher sections of the song I wasn't screeching. Quite often I screeched through many of the songs. I attempted to locate songs on YouTube that offered low key karaoke, and often they were so hard to follow that the singing portion of our services were sorely lacking, or downright horrible!

We began to pray for help with the music. A piano player or someone to play the three guitars Ed had acquired. Someone to lead or help us out was our prayer. We prayed believing God would surely provide.

First would arrive a few soprano singers. Those ladies with their ability to carry those high notes without the chalkboard fingernail screeching that would flow from my voice when pressed too high. Drema could carry those super high notes that few could get and added a layer of harmony that these old hymns needed. I could hear throughout the congregation others that could sing and would later join us when the time came to create a choir. Actually, a vocal ensemble as a choir would require ten, we fluctuated at around four to eight at the beginning.

We were offered a piano that we quickly made arrangements to pick up. It was a nice upright and sounded pretty good. Immediately after the piano was brought in, Ed was asked to preach at a local church on Friday night of their revival. It was there we met Barb! Barb would become our regular piano player, and not only would she play but she would delight us with the flow of the Holy Spirit when they were happy together.

Shortly after Barb began playing for us we were offered another piano. Barb was given her choice as to which piano she preferred to keep. After her choice was made, a piano tuner came to provide the tuning. Interestingly, he had provided service to the very same piano 11 years prior. During that visit he shared with us that a similar story of a man having been given a dream, and opened an old church in Parkersburg. We were quickly reminded that God is doing a special work in gathering HIS elect together for HIS purpose, not just in Frametown but other areas were experiencing the same unique direction of the Holy Spirit.

As us girls began to gather and practice, we would begin to offer to the congregation some good old-fashioned gospel singing, often with three- or four-part harmony. Each week the folks would comment on how good we sounded. We really had such a great time practicing and certainly when Sunday afternoon would roll around, we were thrilled to offer our praise and worship to the Lord.

This time of singing and real enjoyment both by the singers and those attending, brought about the idea of a Gospel Music Gathering. We reached out to those in charge of the Frametown Community Building. This provided the perfect location for us to put on a sing and provide a meal for those attending. This was designed to be a community outreach and ministry to those who are unchurch or possibly those that come to the pantry but might not want to come to a church event.

These events were the bomb!! We reached out to a few local groups that provide good gospel music and set the date and time. We have tried a couple of different ideas for providing food. Offering either potluck or a full meal made, plated and served by Spruce Grove Church. Either way worked well and many folks came out to enjoy the blessing of food, fellowship and really good gospel music.

We have lots of ideas of what our future might hold. We have a handful of teens that are all homeschooled so offering a co-op for homeschoolers is clearly a need for our community. Gathering for educational events, praise and worship events, traveling to areas such as The Ark are all things we keep in mind and stay active as a family of believers, not just worshiping together a few times a week but we are growing together. Truly loving, caring, and praying for one another.

"A new commandment I give to you, that you love one another: just as I have loved you, you also are to love one another." John 13:34

Baptism view

July 4th 2021 service

Fall trip to the Ark – Nov 2022

Part V
The Beginning of God's Magnificence!

Feeding People - God Style

HOW OFTEN DO we hesitate to do something because we think within the limits our own mind, our own ability and stop short of seeing God's glory shine through? God wants to totally show off what HE can do when we allow Him. When we step outside of our own comfort zone and trust and obey, then HE can do things in a way that only God can. When He told me to feed people I moved into the role of operating a food pantry. But when God showed up, though the actions of our obedience, the windows of heaven would open, the flow of abundance would become a regular event.

I would quickly learn the ropes at Mountaineer Food Bank. Their products were set up in two separate ways, and I found the most economical way to stock my shelves. One thing I learned very quickly; I loved having full shelves. Getting new products is always a joy, but keeping full shelves is not the goal. The goal is to have a rotation of product. New items need to come in as the older food goes out. Several times the shelves would get pretty bare. I would stand in front of the shelves and pray to our Heavenly Father. "Lord, you have called me to feed people. I am following your instructions, and I am so thankful for every opportunity. Lord our shelves are getting low, but the need continues to grow. We have many families that have need of our support and help and I trust in You to provide." I do not exaggerate when I say, my shelves do not stay empty or bare for long. We have had unexpected donations come out nowhere. My absolute favorite would be when the mystery pallets would become available at the food bank.

The first time these showed up on my purchase list I had to inquire about them. The listing states "bulk pallet – assorted food". I would soon find out that this would be a pallet I could purchase. Each one had a variety of items from a particular retail store where they had pulled items close to expiration or packages that have been damaged. This entire pallet would be purchased at their low per pound rate. It felt like Christmas morning as we began to go through these boxes. Our shelves would quickly fill up with a huge variety of items that normally wouldn't be available or ones that I had never thought about purchasing but were always enjoyed by those coming through the pantry.

Almost immediately upon getting signed up as a pantry I inquired about the USDA program. The USDA program makes free foods available to approved pantries to give out to those in need in the community. I was told that I needed to get familiar with the process before I would be allowed to sign up for the TFAB (USDA) program. It would be over a year later that I was finally approved to get these products. Much paperwork would be required to offer these foods, which didn't intimidate me in the least. Having additional products was the goal. Around the same time I was able to sign up on the USDA program they ask if I would be interested in getting regular "retail" foods. Our local Walmart would pull all the expiring food from their produce, meats, and bakery shelves. The food bank would pick up those items, and then they would create a schedule for the local pantries to pick up. This was an amazing game changer for our pantry, enabling us to now offer more products and provide for the needs in our area of Braxton county.

Initially, we would set up a few tables in our tiny pantry space. This allowed very little room to move around but worked for the first few times. Then we exploded! Not only with additional foods; but the word was getting out quickly and many local residents began to show up on pantry days. The wonderful thing about retail pantry day is we never knew what items would fill our tables and freezers. We could pick up a few boxes or we could return to the pantry with a fully loaded trailer. Ed and I began to get excited on those pantry days knowing that God always went before us in providing for the needs of this community. He had placed us here and clearly called us to "feed people".

Not sure why, but every time we traveled over a particular portion of interstate 79, going over a bridge and ready to taking the off ramp at the Sutton – Gassaway exit, I had an overwhelming thankfulness towards the 12-foot cargo trailer used to haul the weekly pantry items. I would get weepy and declare thanks and gratitude to our amazing God. As previously mentioned, we purchased the trailer to transport our tools and necessities from Savannah to Frametown. However, our amazing God has gone before us and knew that we would need this trailer for more than our tools. No matter the weather, we now had the perfect provision for hauling loads of food, often more than 1200 pounds, to our little pantry.

Our pantry is outfitted with two freezers. The first freezer can also be a refrigerator with the pressing of a few buttons. It could either freeze food or keep foods cold for fresh items. Most often I would use it as a freezer. Also, we were also gifted a large chest freezer (Thank you Randy and Kathy) that has allowed for overflow of extras to stock away. The top of the chest freezer has often doubled as a shelf on pantry days when we experienced abundance. More times than I can count, we have been blessed with an abundance of meats and other freezer items that the top of the chest freezer could not hold. We simply had no room in either freezer for overflow items. What a blessing to exceed freezer space!

"Bring ye all the tithes into the storehouse, that there may be meat in mine house, and prove me now herewith, saith the LORD of hosts, if I will not open you the windows of heaven, and pour you out a blessing, that there shall not be room enough to receive it." Malachi 3:10

"Feed People"

This is exactly how God began to work, week after week we had an abundance of foods that would overstock our pantry. The excess wasn't because we were not giving it out, not by any means. We always served the many families that came through the pantry on our scheduled days, as well as those stopping in with emergency needs. Often we would deliver the food to those in our community who weren't able to come to our pantry.

What we were receiving on our retail pantry days were those produce items that were near expiration. Fruits and vegetables that were still able to be used but for the purpose of being on a store shelf have passed their salability. This offered us a huge opportunity to provide what would normally be too expensive for many families to purchase. I quickly found out that the cuts of meats that were filling my freezers were those pricier cuts, like the free range organic chicken cuts, thick steaks or pork chops. Most families were unable to purchase in the stores because of the cost, so we were thankful to fill our pantry freezers with these cuts of meat for our community. What a blessing to be able to hand someone a package of ribeye steaks, or a large family-size package of pork chops or even a whole chicken. Being able to offer several packages of nice meats each week was truly a blessing from God himself.

I reflect back on those first ideas, those thoughts in my mind of feeding the homeless population in Savannah Georgia. Now I realize so very clearly that my amazing God with His infinite wisdom had a different plan, had gone before me, and selected this rural area of West Virginia. His plan was to provide for the needs of this resilient, determined and often very proud type of people. One very particular memory will forever solidify God's foreknowledge of making this rural area the location for us to "feed people".

It wasn't long after we began to offer the produce from Walmart that I would find a special friend standing in my pantry. With her hand reaching out towards me, she made a statement that would set in stone why God brought us to Braxton County, West Virginia. Looking up into my face, she stood before me and softly spoke words that revealed to me the cares and concerns of so many in this area. Inside the palm of that slightly shaking hand was a beautiful red apple. She began to tell me that such items as that delicious apple were not always chosen to be purchased when making her weekly trips to the store. "These are so expensive in the stores that it's hard for me to afford them." This singular, red apple was a special treat to this elderly woman who knew full well how to squeeze a budget and get all she could from every single penny. She had spent a lifetime making sacrifices to ensure her home and finances were in order, and knew the current average cost of $1.59 a pound for apples was over the limit. I have to say this shook me, and even as I write, it still moves my heart. To pass up purchasing an apple because it's hard to afford goes much deeper than the per pound price of apples.

Daily, this retired generation on a fixed income struggles to afford even the bare basics. The price of medicine, food, gas, and utilities have skyrocketed in the last few years. When our pantry first opened, we were not able to provide fresh produce, expensive cuts of meats, and other staples to the retired in our community. Also, we needed to help families where only one worked while the other cared for the children or where illness has created a situation where the decision to work was not an option. Another major concern in our community, is the grandparents who seek help because they have taken on the responsibility of caring for their grandchildren, due to the suffering of addiction in the lives of their children.

THIS is where God intended for us to serve. These precious people are the ones God sent us to assist and to offer some support in their daily lives. We help lift a small burden off their budgets so that they can feed their loved ones. But believe me when I say our job doesn't end with the availability of food. God has placed in our hearts a desire to "tend to His sheep." (John 21:16) There is a deep longing in our hearts and a passion to share the love of Jesus with each one that enters our ministry.

In fact, they don't have to enter the doors or our ministry for the same God-given compassion. On many occasions I have looked around and found my husband in Walmart, or the gas station either kneeling to get eye to eye with someone in their car, or with his hand on a shoulder praying with a soul in need of comfort. Several times, after we have finished our morning devotions, we have asked God to bring someone in our path that day so we could be a witness. Having read the book "A Jabez Prayer", we took to heart the concept of asking God to extend our borders. We asked our Father for an opportunity to be a light, to share the Word, and to extend the love of Jesus. We know that He will answer that prayer and place someone with a need of HIM in our day because of His great love for His creation.

God Fulfills His Promise

GOD ADDED A promise with His instruction to me, just as He did Abraham. For Abraham, he would become the father of nations; kings would come from him; and he would become exceedingly fruitful. God's promise to me was not nearly as specific as Abraham's. "Something MAGNIFICENT will happen in that church" can be nearly anything God sets His mind to do. Already in two plus years in making this ministry our life's work, magnificence is all around. Something very special exists within the walls of this little country church. One could consider the many prayers, fellowship, and true brotherly love that existed within the structure of this church having something to do with its continued warmth and inviting feeling. We believe that many angels have been dispatched in the valley to keep watch over the church and offer protection. Their presence lends to that feeling as if you have entered a closer realm to heaven.

Early on we would hear noises, little bumps and banging sounds, coming from the sanctuary. I began to believe that possibly the angels were fluttering about and bouncing off the walls in their joy and excitement. One morning Ed had gone into the sanctuary to pray. He knelt at the altar on the right hand side of the room. As he prayed, eyes closed, he saw a red spot off in the distance of his mind's eye. All of a sudden, this small red spot swooped big and bright before him. Upon opening his eyes, for the briefest moment, he saw a tall, powerful-looking angel standing before him. This angel was bright white, nearly as tall as the ceiling; and his eyes were keenly looking down, watchfully upon my husband. In the smallest snippet of time Ed witnessed this guardian angel watching over him, and just as quickly, the angel was gone.

Directly after this encounter, Ed went down the road to visit our dear friend Dan Reed. Dan had been feeling sick off and on for a few weeks. We would check on him and deliver him food to ensure he was recovering and not requiring medical attention. Although Dan wears hearing implants, he still requires direct face to face conversation to understand every word. They had a brief conversation before Ed prayed over him and his illness. As Ed touched him, Dan bounced back and said "It's all over you! The Holy Spirit is all over you!!" The following day Dan rejoiced in feeling completely well from any form of sickness.

Shortly after we opened the church and began having worship services, a few voiced their interest in having Bible studies. Since Ed was already working and preparing a Sunday sermon, I would work to prepare the Wednesday night Bible studies. I felt as if I had found my niche in teaching Bible lessons. I loved every bit of the process of studying, preparing, and presenting material for a better understanding of the Word of God. We first started with the Gospel of John and then progressed into a study of Ephesians. Later, I created a whole series I called "Back to Basics."

We were informed early on by other ministers that "discipleship" was nearly nonexistent in this area. People would pass down knowledge of the Bible, which was not really based on scripture but more so on hearsay, to their children and grandchildren. We began to see huge holes in Biblical understanding in many of the people who attended our church. This was the basic reason why we started at "In the beginning" and covered many of the main stories to develop a greater understanding of who God is and HIS ultimate plan for mankind, the masterpiece of His creation.

We had a wonderful time studying. My knowledge increased as I prepared; and I was overjoyed as I watched the light bulb come on, so to speak, in the eyes of people. Everything began to come together. Everyone started to understand God's plan from the moment of Adam's first sin, to the cross, and how God had created a plan to redeem those He loves. It was at this time that I came across the book, "Revealing Revelations", by Amir Tsarfati. This book opened the door to offering a Bible study on the book of Revelations. Immediately, within the first few verses of the book of Revelations, a beautiful promise is declared. ***"Blessed is he who reads and those who hear the words of this prophecy, and keeps those things which are written in it, for the time is near." Revelations 1:3***. This was reason enough for me to pursue the challenge of studying this book. The study material offered by Amir made the challenge much easier because all previous studies, up to that point, were ones I had created in my own time of study and preparation.

Upon finishing class one evening, several of the ladies hung around for a time of fellowship. As I walked them out the front door, there was a wonderful fragrance that filled the air. The aroma was like the most diverse bouquet of fragrant flowers: roses, lilies, gardenias, and lilacs. Not one flower stood out but a combination or even a fragrance from a flower we do not have here on earth. It was sweet and pleasant yet thick in the air. I immediately commented about the sweetness that filled the air. The other ladies could smell it as well; one even bent down to smell the new fall arrangements I had just purchased that day, and which sat on each side of the porch stairs. I had plans of using them to fill the front entrance urns. As you know, fall flowers generally do not offer a pleasant smell. In fact, mums are designed to repel insects rather than drawing them in; unlike the sweetness of summer flowers which draws in the bees and other nectar seeking insects. There was nothing in the area that would justify the beautiful fragrance that we experienced as we said our goodbyes that evening.

The smell lingered in my nose and created a special memory. I shared my experience with my family on our group messaging, as I felt the fragrance was another visitation from heavenly places. But it was when I awoke early the following morning to that very same fragrance that I knew this was a special visit intended just for me. That same wonderful aroma I witnessed on the front porch the previous evening was now in my bedroom in the early morning hours. Maybe it was an angel visitation, or maybe it was Jesus himself who came to my home. I felt honored at the Heavenly presence which filled my head with this wonderful, sweet fragrance.

This made me think of the time Mary anointed Jesus' feet with the spikenard ointment. The fragrance filled the whole house, and everyone was blessed with this gift she offered Him with her sacrifice of worship. I have often visualized Mary wiping His feet with her hair. What an intimate time of worship and honoring of the Savior she loved so much. I am convinced that Mary's hair would have carried that fragrance for days if not weeks. I can picture her brushing her hair and holding the ends up to her nose, inhaling deeply the sweet fragrance, cherishing this wonderful memory, and adding a treasure to her heart.

Souls are being saved and redeemed through the work at Spruce Grove Church. A man who had been in prison for eight years for an unspeakable crime sat through a Wednesday night Bible study one evening. It was near the time of Easter, so we were covering some details surrounding Jesus going to the cross. Near the end we showed a short video clip of Barabbas. This video showed how Jesus loved him, just as he loves you and me. Near the end of the video Ed could hear the sounds of sniffling and shallow sobs. Having finished the class, Ed accompanied this man to the front porch. It was there he presented a question to Ed that he would never forget. "Do

God Fulfills His Promise

you think Jesus could forgive me?" Ed had been counseling this young man for several months. They had sat on that same porch when he told Ed those horrible things that had put him in prison. Ed knew when this man was asking if Jesus could forgive him that this was not a small question. Ed spent a few minutes sharing how much Jesus loved him, just as he loved Barabbas from the video. "Yes, Jesus loves YOU! No sin is too great for His love." It wasn't long until these two men walked back into the church, knelt at the altar, and this man gave his heart to Jesus. He asked for Jesus to forgive him of his sins; and Jesus did, as He always does, and redeemed him from even the worst of sins.

Our area of the county is blessed with a sweet young man by the name of Zach. Zach has never met a stranger because he has such a huge, loving personality. Zach also has cerebral palsy which creates difficulty for him to perform many daily tasks. His precious body twists and turns and prevents him from speaking clearly as well as preventing full movement with his hands. Zach doesn't miss a lick when it comes to his thoughts. He is sharp, aware, and tries to express his care and concern for those around him. Zach had always wanted to get baptized, but his previous pastor said he didn't need to. This is probably a true statement since there is not a more kind and loving soul on the earth. Zach has a genuine innocence that comes with certain conditions. However, he had a longing in his heart to be baptized.

We got to know Zach during our first vacation Bible school. He was here every day, and immediately Zach and Ed became best of friends. Ed would call out, "My Man!" and Zach would repeat it. They were fast friends. That week Zach began to tell Ed that he desired to be baptized. He had witnessed many baptisms and inquired why they would get put under the water. Finally, Zach realized that it was to show their love for Jesus. We put Zach's name on the list for our first baptism. Zach's family informed Pastor Ed that because Zach didn't have the ability to fully close his mouth that instead of going backwards into the water, he would need to be put forward. Ed took all the instructions and took exceptional care of his precious friend. They entered the water that beautiful summer day.

Standing in the deepest part of the backed-up creek, Ed asked Zach if he loved Jesus. He quickly and clearly stated "YES." Ed proceeded with "I baptize you in the name of the Father, the Son, and the Holy Spirit" and leaned him forward. Instead of allowing himself to be dunked in the water, Zach took off swimming. Quickly Ed took one step forward, put his hand on Zach's head, and dunked him under the water and just as quickly Ed retrieved him up out of the water. The crowd cheered and laughed at the same time at this not-so-by-the-book baptism. Since then, every time baptism has been brought up in our church, Zach quickly reminds everyone that he has been baptized! He has completed what the Word of God has instructed; being saved and baptized.

"Go therefore and make disciples of all the nations, baptizing them in the name of the Father and of the Son and of the Holy Spirit, teaching them to observe all things that I have commanded you" Matthew 28:19-20a

Ed and Zach working together on pantry day

Zack: Spruce Grove Church's official bell ringer

Zach's baptism was definitely one to remember but another one also comes to my mind as equally precious. We had a family that began to attend our services on a regular basis. They attended for several months without much discussion about where they stood in their relationship with the Lord. Then one Wednesday after Bible study, Eric announced he has never received salvation. We discussed in more detail exactly what that involved. They went home that evening without the decision to pray. We now had a better understanding of Eric's heart, and we continued to pray for his decision to accept Jesus. The following Sunday the entire service would go by without Eric making his way to the altar. However, just as the service ended, Eric approached Ed and asked if he would pray with him. Together they knelt at the altar, and Ed led him in a sinner's prayer. I have no doubt of the heart-felt confession Eric gave the Lord that day. He took his time to gain knowledge and understanding of what it meant to follow Jesus during those months they had been attending our church. When Eric made that walk to the altar, it was a man who had been shown the light, directly from his Heavenly Father, as he offered his heart to Jesus.

Personally, I will never forget watching Eric get up from that precious time in prayer. The man glowed! He beamed from having met the Heavenly Father in a time of confession and acceptance of the blood of Jesus that had been shed for his sins. The day that was scheduled for Eric's baptism was a stormy late winter day. Throughout the entire Sunday service there was heavy rain and thunder. Eric went to the pulpit to give his testimony of how God had begun working on him through his daughter's desire for him to be in church. He stated that when he first came, he had a bit of an attitude and was uncertain of all that was being taught. Yet God began to reveal Himself to Eric and that changed everything. He chose a passage of scripture to read during his testimony.

God Fulfills His Promise

"For we ourselves were also once foolish, disobedient, deceived, serving various lusts and pleasures, living in malice and envy, hateful and hating one another. But when the kindness and the love of God our Savior towards man appeared, not by works of righteousness which we have done but according to His mercy He saved us, through the washing of regeneration and renewing of the Holy Spirit, whom He poured out on us abundantly through Jesus Christ our Savior." Titus 3:2-7

I kid you not, when Eric spoke these words, the thunder clapped so loudly that the building shook. Almighty God was present and included His confirmation, making clear the words Eric was reading were true and chosen perfectly for the day. God had been present and was watching every single moment of that day's events. When Eric finished his testimony, we gathered our umbrellas and headed for the creek. I grabbed the portable speaker that would allow us to listen to Bluetooth music so that a selection of music would be elevated throughout the valley. Thus we witnessed another expression of faith in a new believer. The selection chosen was "Baptized" by Zack Williams.

Every time I hear this song, I think of our friend Eric giving his testimony with a huge Amen from the Heavens. We were rejoicing with the angels. What a precious time for the Lord this little church in the valley had seen in a short period of time. The Lord's magnificence doesn't end with salvation and baptisms. We believe in the healing power of the blood of Jesus Christ. Many times, we have laid hands on someone who came forward, and later he or she returned with reports of being fully restored to health. We have witnessed healings of bad hearts, bad backs, kidney malfunctions, and colon concerns.

Time after time we have followed the instructions of the scriptures by gathering the elders together and anointing with oil those who are ill. Many times right there as we prayed, we experienced the powerful presence of the Holy Spirit, and many people have walked away knowing they have been touched, healed, or have received the power of the Blood of Jesus Christ.

"Prayer of a righteous man avails much." James 5:14

Within the first few months of starting the ministry in Frametown we were called out to minister to a young couple that had spent nearly ten years of their young lives in addiction. We were directed to the highest point of Calhoun county where we sat on a front porch with a beautiful view and shared our testimony of redemption. Ed poured his heart out to this young couple that afternoon. Speaking their language, they understood exactly where he came from. Ed shared how he lost access to his sons' lives because of addiction. Also, he had lost relationships, jobs, money, and everything else because of his nearly thirty years in this drugged state. But Ed pointed out that TODAY was the day they could be free from this addictive habit that has such an ugly hold on their lives. They had heard the stories of their addicted cousin, the lost and wandering black sheep of the family. However, this man that sat before them that afternoon, eye to eye, was no longer the man they had previously heard about. This man was sharing freedom with them, and HOPE showed up that day and took a front row seat on that porch. The smallest amount of hope can be all it takes to see one's way out of the darkness. We helped them find a treatment program, and although they didn't fully embrace everything offered immediately, within a few more weeks every word spoken high on that mountain top would ring TRUTH in their ears. Over and over again they began to truly believe they could find the same freedom.

God Fulfills His Promise

Today as I write this, this beautiful couple is celebrating two years clean and sober. They have restored lives, restored relationships, and restored health and vitality. They have chosen to work in the recovery profession where they occasionally hit the streets with the message to those who are still sick and suffering from addiction. No longer looking for their own high but seeking out that lost soul willing to hear about this man named Jesus. How He came into this world to save those who are lost, broken, and hurt. Jesus restored my husband to the brilliant, powerful man of God he was born and intended to be. Jesus is restoring this sweet couple, so they can live a full and amazing life FREE from drugs and alcohol. Now, this couple share their testimony which becomes strength and hope to others that are still in the struggle.

Staying the Course

GOD IS STILL writing the rest of this story of the work being done in Spruce Grove Church in little Frametown, West Virginia. God's plan is far from being finished as we continue the work He set out for us to accomplish. But through the process I have many times wondered, was this God's plan all along for my life? All those years of wandering around with a few spurts of small successes. Just enough to keep me going. And for Ed? My goodness that man has been through decades of disappointments. Decades of failed relationships, jobs, years of total destruction. Then we meet and through the mighty hand of God things begin to fall into place. Our lives now firmly planted into a work that has purpose, God's purpose. We have a dear friend who says, "When God is in it, there is no limit!" We know for certain this is HIS ministry. HIS calling upon our lives. HIS orchestration placed us exactly where HE wanted.

Our Heavenly Father with His constant, watchful eye looked down upon those two drunk kids swaying to the sounds of Amazing Grace decided He could put into action the words of verse two:

> *'Twas grace that taught my heart to fear*
> *And grace, my fears relieved*
> *How precious did that grace appear*
> *The hour I first believed*

Through His amazing grace we began to believe again. Believe that we could allow ourselves to dream. Again. Believe that through the molding of God's mighty hand we might live, truly live and not just survive. Believing is a powerful, heartfelt step in the direction of trusting in God's love and mercy.

These last few years we have seen amazing successes, great stories of how God has worked and provided, and changed lives, not just our own but many lives, in whom we been able to minister. But do not let that fool you into believing it has been easy. Not by a long shot! The work of rehabbing this old church building presented its own set of challenges and certainly required most of our savings to see an old, neglected building come to life. Then there were the emotional and spiritual challenges.

I have often stated, God threw us in the deep end of the ministerial pool. I recall that sense of urgency to get the ball rolling and here we are, having dove head and heart first into the ministry that God designed just for us. This is not the typical path travelled by most entering ministry. We would receive our ordination through The Missionary Church International which recognized those called into ministry in a non-conventional way. They recognize those involved in "parachurch" ministry. A parachurch is a Christian organization that operates outside or beside a specific religious denomination or local church. Engaged in social welfare, such as feeding people and caring for those in addiction, with a goal of sharing the gospel and evangelizing those within our reach. Basically, doing all that a regular minister involved in any particular denomination would do, we just happened to be going at it under the guidance and direction of our Heavenly Father. For that purpose we keep close to us several mentors who are available for guidance and willingness to pray with us over difficult issues that might arise.

Our journey is just beginning. This is not just our journey but is wound tightly around the Father's will. We are determined to dive deeper every day into the Word for further Truth, understanding, and greater gifts. We know He has hand picked us for this location to serve the people in this community. We have faced various trials and even a few demonic attacks sent our way in an attempt at discouraging or destroying our efforts.

I can recall one in particular with a timeframe of fall 2021. I was kept up night after night feeling as if I was being watched or taunted. I would pray for the release of these dark spirits wanting to tease and pull at me, yet for nearly a week I was getting no real relief or traction over this very clear demonic attack. Until I went on the offense. I knew the very moment the dark spirit tucked its tail and left. I had found the key to its release in the scriptures and have not felt the pressure since.

As Christians we must be aware that we have an enemy that "accuses the brethren day and night" (Revelations 12:10) The enemy seeks to steal, kill and destroy and will stop at nothing to see that accomplished. In fact we have had many conversations on how the devil was trying to take us out throughout our lifetime. Ed's life specifically has been plagued with many events from unexplained childhood illness sending him into extreme fevers and convulsions. Shadowy figures in his bedroom doorway and chemical abuse starting at the young age of five. These evil spirits tracking his every move to destroy him, knowing that should God get ahold of his life, he would have a level of compassion for the lost and speak boldly to see individuals come to Christ.

As we draw closer to our Heavenly Father we know that He has been aware and goes before us to prepare and plan our path. Especially once we have given him our all and allowed His full rein and guidance in our life. This gives me great comfort, especially in the times of difficulty when I know my Father has gone before me and whatever situation, both good and bad, has been sifted through His hands prior to it entering my life. Just recently, I experienced a time of difficulty. Through that moment I was able to learn a valuable lesson and immediately use that very lesson to help a brother through a similar dark moment.

We had returned from a short visit to Moravian Falls, North Carolina. During our visit, wonderful connections and communications with the

Lord filled our time. A few days after returning home, I felt like I was a million miles away from God's presence. I prayed and read scripture and even once planted my face in the carpet beside my bed crying out to the Lord to feel His presence. It was at this time of intense groaning before the Lord that scripture began to flow through me. "The Lord Himself goes before you; He will be with you. He will never leave you nor forsake you. Do not be afraid or discouraged." Deuteronomy 31:8 I began to declare to the Lord, "I don't have to feel your presence Lord, I don't have to hear your sweet voice. I fully believe everything written in the Word of God that says it's not based on my situation, circumstance or feelings. My salvation is in my faith and trust in my mighty God. My faith and belief is in Jesus Christ who came to this world to redeem me from my sins and my sins are washed in the blood of the Lamb." I continued with declarations of what I know the scriptures says about me as a child of God. I am blessed, I am redeemed, I am loved, I am His. I went on and on with what I know from the scriptures. This is belief regardless of feeling or circumstances and where I rest my faith.

A few months later I am standing in the living room of one of our dear saints that attends our church. His precious daughter had just died from an apparent drug overdose. Sitting in the same room was his son, brother to the deceased young woman. As he stood up and prepared to leave, he stated, "I really cannot see God in any of this". He informed us that his wife and children were all at home with the stomach virus that had been plaguing our area for the last few months. Everything about his world was dark and ugly. Immediately I was able to draw upon my moment of being face down into that blue carpet at home. I reflected that it's not in our circumstances or how we might feel, it's in our faith. This is the time when all we can do is stand. Stand in the knowledge that God's word is truth. God's word is to be trusted. God is aware and fully engaged in those dark days we must face. As I prayed with him, asking for God's peace and comfort to come upon him and his family, I ask that God's word would be truth in his heart and mind, that no matter how distant God may feel, He never leaves, never forsakes and is carrying him through this dark time in their family's life. I know God heard my prayer. I know that broken man of God that I prayed over was renewed in peace and comfort and would one day look back and know that God was beside him every step of the way.

These stories I have shared with you, are just a few of the many ways God is working. As we develop our Christian walk and continue training in the Word of God and offer a willingness to follow him, we are seeing miracles happen. We are seeing lives change. We witness people growing in their understanding and in their faith. These are all the results of being aligned with the Heavenly Father on an earthly mission to "go into all the world and preach the gospel to every creature." Mark 16:15

God's Word and His promises are always true and mighty because He is the Creator of all things. When He sets His mind to accomplish something, it will be completed. God has promised "Something magnificent will happen in that little church." Many would argue that magnificent things have already happened, which is quite true. However, I know that something still is yet to happen. God's magnificence is yet to fully pour out upon this little church in the valley. God's greatness is yet to be fully revealed in the purpose for us opening an old church and feeding His people. What has happened is just the beginning. The most exciting part is when He calls upon His children to go into business with Him. As heirs to the Father, we have ownership in the outcome of Heaven; and as joint heirs with Jesus Christ, we have work to do. We are called to enter a joint venture with the great I AM!

"Being confident of this very thing, that He who has begun a good work in you will complete it until the day of Jesus Christ." Philippians 1:6

Progression pictures of Spruce Grove Community Church

August 1st 2020 Arrival day to begin the transformation

Snow covered – January 2022

Well loved – Fall 2022